Practical Activities and Ideas for Parents of Dyslexic Kids and Teens

Practical Activities and Ideas for Parents of Dyslexic Kids and Teens

GAVIN REID, MICHELLE MCINTOSH
and JENN CLARK

Jessica Kingsley Publishers
London and Philadelphia

First published in Great Britain in 2022 by Jessica Kingsley Publishers
An Hachette Company

1

Copyright © Gavin Reid, Michelle McIntosh and Jenn Clark 2022

Front cover image source: Shutterstock®. The cover image is for illustrative
purposes only, and any person featuring is a model.

A CIP catalogue record for this title is available from the British Library and the Library of Congress

ISBN 978 1 78775 761 5
eISBN 978 1 78775 762 2

Printed and bound in Great Britain by Bell & Bain Limited

Jessica Kingsley Publishers' policy is to use papers that are natural, renewable and recyclable
products and made from wood grown in sustainable forests. The logging and manufacturing
processes are expected to conform to the environmental regulations of the country of origin.

Jessica Kingsley Publishers
Carmelite House
50 Victoria Embankment
London EC4Y 0DZ

www.jkp.com

Contents

Acknowledgements

We would like to acknowledge our students past and present who helped shape our ideas and activities for this book and, of course, their parents and families with whom we have worked closely. They have all brightened our daily work and enriched our practice.

We would also like to acknowledge one of our students, Kiera Loverin, who has a long-standing passion for visual arts and has a dual diagnosis of dyslexia and giftedness. She is Tlingit and Tahltan First Nations and lives in Vancouver, Canada, and contributed a number of the illustrations for this book. She is proud to say this is her first book illustration project.

Preface

Welcome to this activity book for parents of children and young people with dyslexia. We are delighted to be given the opportunity to write this book and we have enjoyed the process very much. We are all very experienced in supporting children and families in a number of capacities and fully appreciate the issues and dilemmas faced by parents and carers of children and young people with dyslexia. These issues have taken on a great intensity due to the COVID-19 pandemic and the increase in home tutoring and remote teaching.

Irrespective of this, it is important that parents are equipped to provide activities and develop and monitor their child's progress. Although this is obviously carried out in conjunction with the school, it is nevertheless an important role for parents.

In our respective roles as parents, teachers and psychologists, we have developed these activities, using our experiences, with the prime purpose of supporting parents and helping them support their children. We have made the activities accessible and interesting; they are also varied and we have incorporated the key areas of need for children and young people with dyslexia: reading, writing, spelling, social and emotional issues, executive functioning and learning skills. We have endeavoured to provide a stimulating and comprehensive range of activities for the learners.

Ideally, we are attempting to promote self-sufficiency in learning but for children with dyslexia this is extremely challenging. We have therefore provided follow-up exercises and teaching tips to help parents take their child through the activities without pain or tears! We appreciate that frustration and sometimes avoidance are features of the child with dyslexia and we hope the activities will stimulate and engage the young person and thereby play a part in promoting self-learning.

It is our sincere hope that this book is a welcome source of support for parents and provides children with stimulating activities that make learning engaging and fun! We have also included a section on social and emotional issues as our experiences tell us that a happy learner is a successful learner! We hope this book brings some happiness to parents and children!

Gavin Reid, Michelle McIntosh, Jenn Clark
March 2021

How to Use this Book

We would like to give you some advice on how to use this book although we are sure that it is very straightforward and you will be able to access the ideas and strategies very well.

We have divided the book into chapters, each dealing with an important area to help you access the information you need easily. As well as areas such as reading, spelling and writing, we have also included executive functioning, social and emotional factors and learning skills. It is too easy for these three areas to be overlooked as literacy is usually prioritized, and these terms will be explained in the chapters that follow.

There is no right order to progress through the book. It is very much a 'dip in' book and you can start wherever you want. We have tried to cater for a broad range of ages and provided a clear focus on how you as a parent can use these activities with your child.

The first chapter provides an overview of dyslexia and this will likely answer the questions we find parents often ask, such as what is dyslexia and how can I as a parent help my child?

We have introduced each activity with a comment usually indicating why the activity is important and how the activity can be carried out. There is also an approximate time you should put aside for the activity.

We have also indicated any preparation that might be necessary before starting the activity, and included some additional points such as teaching tips and the word toolbox. The word toolbox will help your child build up a bank of words and consolidate what they have accomplished in the activity. The idea is that you can help your child think of new words they have come across in the activity and put them into a 'word toolbox' with the meaning. They can draw their own word toolbox for each activity and insert their own words. The icon is there as a reminder.

We have suggested in some of the activities that children keep a chart of what they have learned that day. If you wish, you can use the prompt, 'What have I learned today?' for each activity. This will be their own record of what they have done. We have also included some follow-up activities or websites. You will find additional resources for some of the activities in the Appendix. These resources are available to photocopy and download at: www.jkp.com/catalogue/book/9781787757615. Useful websites are listed in the 'Further Information' section at the end of the book.

We have tried to make this book very accessible and appealing to the child and of course to you as a parent. We do hope it will be motivating and engaging for learners and will help you engage more fully in your child's learning. We appreciate that remote learning and working at home has become a more realistic and sometimes a necessary factor and we hope this book will help you and your child to enjoy working together and to achieve a sense of accomplishment.

CHAPTER 1

About Dyslexia

Introduction

As a parent of a child(ren) or young adult with dyslexia, the first questions you have are likely to be:

- What is dyslexia?
- How can I help?

This will in time lead to other questions, such as:

- Will my child improve?
- What kind of progress can I expect?
- What are the future study and career implications?

It is right that you should be asking those questions. We find in our daily practice as literacy tutors, trainers and assessors that those are exactly the questions parents ask. As an introduction to this activity book we feel it is helpful, and certainly appropriate, to provide some responses to those questions.

This introductory chapter provides an overview of the area of dyslexia and we include the range of characteristics of dyslexia, some current research and what you might expect from an assessment and subsequent diagnosis. We also consider identification and intervention and specifically the barriers children and parents experience, and the impact of those on the family and the child. We focus a great deal on the strengths children with dyslexia display. This is very important as it helps to maintain self-esteem, which is a crucial element in any intervention programme. We want the young person to feel good after an activity so it is important to provide the right type of structure and lead-in to any activity or task.

The activities in this book highlight the positive aspects of dyslexia and particularly how we as parents and teachers can help the learner identify and build on their strengths as well as help them deal with the challenges they experience.

Background

Literacy

The prevalent view of dyslexia is that it relates to difficulties in acquiring literacy and particularly acquiring competence in phonological processing – that is, recognizing the sounds in words and relating these to the visual symbol (the letter/s). Many of the activities in Chapter 2 will focus on different aspects of phonological processing. The importance of phonological processing has been derived from substantial evidence that difficulties in this area, particularly when related to reading, have been a major distinguishing factor between dyslexics and non-dyslexics from early literacy learning to adulthood (you may want to look at the Rose Report 2009 for information on this). This therefore is a key area for intervention, and all aspects of phonological and phonemic instruction need to be prioritized (this involves teaching children how to use letter–sound relations to read and spell words). Some researchers suggest that teaching phonemic awareness, when linked to teaching systematic decoding and spelling, is a key to preventing failure in children who come to school without these prerequisite skills. In the UK, the Rose Report (2009) recommended that high-quality systematic phonics should be taught as the prime approach in learning to read.

Research has highlighted five key aspects for teaching reading. These are shown below and will be included in the activities throughout this book.

1. **Phonological awareness** – recognizing individual sounds and sound combinations in words.
2. **Phonics** – recognizing the letters and letter combinations that make sounds and matching the visual symbol (letters) to the sounds. This is important for spelling.
3. **Fluency** – being able to read without too many hesitations or skipping words. This is important for comprehension.
4. **Vocabulary** – this is often an issue with adults as they have not assimilated a working vocabulary so reading is not automatic. This means they have to stop when they come across an unknown word. This has an impact on comprehension.
5. **Comprehension** – this provides a purpose for reading and includes both literal comprehension and inferential comprehension (reading between the lines).

In addition to reading, we also need to consider other aspects of literacy such as writing and spelling. There is evidence that the strategies used to develop phonological skills are also necessary for spelling. Although there are many other skills required for spelling, understanding the correspondences between sounds and letters needs to be prioritized. There are a large number of exceptions to the rules, and a lack of predictability in spelling but it is estimated that around 50 per cent of words do follow a predictable pattern based on sound–letter correspondence.[1] We therefore include activities on spelling in this book. Spelling is also important for expressive writing. We find that many children with dyslexia are reluctant writers because they have a fear of spelling. Although the use of technology has helped children and young people with dyslexia, they may still have considerable issues putting their thoughts down on paper.

Cognitive skills

Cognition might seem a confusing and intimidating term to some, but it simply refers to how we process information. Dyslexia can be referred to as a processing difference and this is because children and young people with dyslexia may have a difficulty at various stages of the information processing cycle. This cycle refers to how we take information in – visually, through listening (auditory), kinesthetic (through experience) and tactile (through touch).

The evidence points to the view that children with dyslexia need intervention using a multisensory approach – that means that all of the above need to be engaged when we are teaching them.

Cognitive skills also include attention, memory and comprehension. It is important that these aspects are addressed and we have included activities on these in this book.

Other aspects such as the environment, social and cultural factors as well as bilingual abilities can also impact on the outcomes of the learning experience. The environment includes the learning context in the classroom, the school, the community and the home, and this has an influence on both learning and teaching. It is important to consider the individual learning and cultural preferences in order to provide a supportive environment for effective learning as well as the emotional needs of children with dyslexia.

Identification – barriers experienced by children with dyslexia

There are some core characteristics of dyslexia that are important for identification and assessment and for the development of education, health and care plans (EHCPs), and teaching and curriculum materials. These characteristics can present considerable barriers to learning for children and young people in school.

It may be helpful to view dyslexia by attempting to identify and address the barriers to literacy and learning that can be experienced by the child. These barriers may also lie within the classroom environment as well as in the nature of the learning task and cognitive challenges associated with learning. Barriers that can be associated with phonological difficulties and decoding include:

---

1   https://dyslexiaida.org/spelling

- Substitution of words when reading aloud words with similar meanings.
- Difficulty with rhyming and remembering the sequence of the rhyme.
- Difficulty with the sequence of the alphabet or the passage.
- Poor word attack skills, particularly with unknown words.
- Slow and hesitant reading speed, often with little expression.

Processing difficulties

These include:

- Poor working memory (short-term memory).
- Difficulty remembering lists of information, even short lists, or short instructions.
- Poor long-term memory and difficulties with organization.
- Difficulty displaying knowledge and understanding – this can result in limitations in written work.
- Difficulties in recalling a sequence of events and organizing information.

The chart below highlights the characteristic difficulties experienced by children with dyslexia and the impact these may have on their learning.

Characteristics	Impact
Phonological awareness/ processing	Difficulty in decoding print, particularly unknown words that cannot be read visually.
Short-term memory	Difficulty in storing information for a short period, such as instructions or when copying information from a book. It can be particularly problematic in maths.
Working memory	This can also be problematic in maths, particularly mental arithmetic. Working memory involves remembering information and undertaking a processing activity at the same time. For example, if the child receives three instructions at the same time this will put a considerable strain on working memory.
Word finding	Difficulty in recalling some words; child uses either the wrong word or gives a long, wordy description of what he/she wants to say.
Processing speed	Challenges with processing speed, taking longer to complete a task. May also lose the track of a problem because it takes a long time to process – often noted in maths.
Organization	Difficulty in organizing thoughts and materials. May forget to bring items to school and need a structure when recording information.
Automaticity	May take longer to achieve consistency and competence in a task. This is because the child will not have automaticity until the skill is practised for a lengthy time. This could be a spelling rule or a new word or a motor task like riding a bike. Learning will take longer to become automatic, and additional time needs to be allowed for this.

The assessment

In the UK, a formal assessment and diagnosis can be made by a specialist teacher assessor[2] or through a practitioner psychologist registered with the Health and Care Professions Council (HCPC).[3]

The assessment can be formal, as conducted by a specialist assessor or a psychologist, or informal and carried out by an experienced and specialist class teacher. Informal assessment does not necessarily provide a diagnosis but can give pointers for intervention. These include percentile, working memory, visual spatial, IQ, general ability, confidence interval, DSM-V, dyslexia, specific learning difficulties and neurodiversity (for more information see Reid and Guise 2019).

It is important that a formal assessment provides information on the tests used and explains the implications of the results. It is also important that an assessment can lead to action and therefore it should provide some guidance for the development of an intervention programme as well as some strategies for parents to use at home. (Katrina Cochrane (2021) has contributed an interesting chapter to Gillian Ashley's book, *Parenting a Dyslexic Child*, that provides details of this – see References at the end of this book).

Linking home and school

Parents have a key role to play in early identification. In many cases, it is the parent who alerts the school to their concerns over the child's literacy development. The parent may actually be aware of concerns before the child even starts school, particularly if there are other children in the family or relatives who have dyslexia. Parents usually know their child well and will be alert to signs of anxiety or stress when the child is learning new material. It is important that there are good links between home and school.

Checklists can't tell you whether a learner is dyslexic. They are useful because they outline your learner's strengths and weaknesses, and can help to inform a supportive teaching strategy. For more information, see the British Dyslexia Association's webpage on checklists for dyslexia, where you can download examples of checklists for children at primary and secondary schools.[4]

About the activities

This introductory chapter has aimed to set the scene for the activities that follow. Each section will have some introductory text to guide you into the activities and provide a context for these.

---

2   https://sasc.org.uk; www.bdadyslexia.org.uk/services/accreditation/dyslexia-assessor-accreditation/ apc-renewal; www.patoss-dyslexia.org/About-Us

3   www.hcpc-uk.org

4   www.bdadyslexia.org.uk/dyslexia/how-is-dyslexia-diagnosed/dyslexia-checklists

You will find there are also sections in each activity for additional resources and we have pinpointed some key websites here that you may want to look at.

It is worth remembering that the activities can also be used as a catalyst for activities you may want to try on that topic – and very importantly one of the aims is to motivate the learner and ideally help them become self-motivated and successful. You will find in the last chapter of this book there is an activity on learning preferences and it might be an idea to look at this first as this can provide some clues to how your child(ren) may learn.

We have tried to make the activities fun and interesting so they will engage your child and spur them to further study and help them to overcome the learning barriers they may experience due to dyslexia.

CHAPTER 2

Reading

I am sure you appreciate that reading is the biggest hurdle children and young people with dyslexia have to deal with. This can be reading accuracy, fluency and/or reading comprehension. We have provided activities on all three here in this chapter. Clearly accuracy is important, although some children with dyslexia become very good at reading using contextual cues or even visual cues. Reliance on these strategies, however, can be fraught and must be treated with some caution. It is important that children with dyslexia acquire the fundamentals of reading – letter and sound recognition and word rules and the manipulation of words for plurals and prefixes and suffixes. Knowing these fundamentals will help them decode new words and this will help with both fluency and comprehension.

We have tried to vary the activities in this chapter and provided at least a sample of most of the main aspects of reading. We hope these activities will help to engage your child in the reading process and help to read for pleasure and enjoyment.

ACTIVITIES

1. Popcorn Reading

Introduction

This activity is a paired reading activity that can be done with parents and children. The goals for this activity are to encourage children to read aloud, become more comfortable with reading aloud and to follow along with the text as the other person is reading. Dyslexic children often struggle with reading and, as such, will avoid reading aloud. This activity can be a fun way to encourage students to practise reading.

Good for...

Any age at which the child can read. This activity is ideal as it can be done with children who are emerging readers and are reading simple books, as well as older children who may be reading a novel with their parent.

Time frame

It is a good idea to dedicate a good 15–20 minutes to this activity and it can be done every day. The more practice the child has with reading aloud, the more comfortable they become and the more fluent they may become as well.

Preparation/Materials

- Your child's current favourite book that they feel comfortable reading
- An actual bowl of popcorn or a printed and laminated copy of the popcorn bowl and printed, cut-out and laminated pieces of popcorn (see the Appendix for a version you can print out)

Teaching tip

In our experience, students who struggle with reading will sometimes only read a very small bit at a time in order to avoid reading too much. This is okay and a way to get around this is to minimize the amount that you read as well to match your child, so as to encourage them to keep reading and keep following along.

Activity

Begin by explaining to your child that you are going to do some popcorn reading. At this time, you can introduce an actual bowl of popcorn or the printed and laminated popcorn bowl and pieces included in this book. Explain to your child that one of you will begin reading the book aloud. The child can choose who begins. At any time during the first person's reading time, they may decide to stop reading and pop a piece of popcorn in their mouth or pass a printed popcorn piece to the other person, at which point the other person will continue reading where the first person left off. The process continues until the reading time is done or the bowl of popcorn is finished!

Follow-up

For children who are not yet reading full passages in books, you can also use word lists that the child is comfortable with and then you and your child can practise reading them 'popcorn style' together.

If you or your child discover new words you don't know or are curious about, write them down on a piece of paper and look them up together at a later time.

Word toolbox

What words did your child learn today? Try to find two new words that you or your child learned and have your child use them in a sentence.

Additional resources

This activity is not encouraged in a classroom setting or with text that the child is not comfortable with. The idea is to allow for your child to become more comfortable reading and reading aloud. It is strongly advised to not use text that is too advanced for them.

2. Mouse and Cheese Reading

Introduction

This is a fun activity that parents can facilitate for their child in order to have them practise recognition of words that the child needs to improve their reading. This is also a good activity to use when we want children to practise high-frequency word recognition as well.

Good for...

Any age at which the student can read. This is a highly customizable activity as the parent can use any words that are at the child's current level or words that are sent home from school for review.

Time frame

This activity can be done in a short amount of time but will be based on the child's reading ability and their ability to find the matching word. Initial preparation time should take around 30 minutes to print and laminate the mouse and cheese pieces and to cut them out (see the Appendix). Actual activity time varies depending on the reader's ability.

Preparation/Materials

- Several printed, laminated and cut-out mouse and cheese pieces. Lamination of the pieces allows you to reuse them several times. Should you not have access to a laminator, the pieces can simply be printed on cardstock each time you want to do the activity. Another option would be to place sticky notes on the pieces as well so that the pieces can be reused
- A dry-erase marker or a regular marker for non-laminated pieces
- A list of words for the child to review
- Sticky notes (should lamination not be possible)

Teaching tip

Due to working memory challenges, sometimes children will read the word initially and then have a hard time finding the matching cheese piece and then completely forget the word they are searching for. You can help your child with this by asking them while they are searching, 'What word are we looking for again?' This will encourage the child to read the word again on the mouse piece and remember what word they are looking for.

Activity

To prepare for this activity, you will need to print the mouse and cheese pieces on heavy paper or cardstock. If you have access to a laminator, you can laminate the pieces. If no laminator is accessible, print off the pieces on heavy cardstock. The pieces will need to be cut out. Once the pieces are ready, write the words to be reviewed on the mouse pieces and then the same words on the printed cheese pieces. Then take the cheese pieces and hide them around the room or around the area where the activity will take place. You then give your child the mouse pieces. Your child has to read the word on the first mouse piece and then find the cheese piece with the matching word that is hidden somewhere around the room or space. Be sure to have your child read the word when they look at the mouse piece *and* when they find the matching cheese piece.

Follow-up

This activity is especially good for high-frequency words and words that are non-phonetic in nature and require quick recognition. Practising these words on a regular basis helps your child automatically decode or read these words, which helps in reading fluency.

Ask your child to use the word in a sentence once they have found the match, to solidify comprehension.

The pieces can also be used in a classic memory-style game by writing the words on each piece and turning them over. Your child can then flip them over one at a time and try to find the match.

Word toolbox

For words that your child struggled with during this activity, have them trace their fingers over the word and say the letters as they trace to help solidify the word in their memory.

Additional resources

See Mouse and Cheese worksheets in the Appendix.

3. Oops!

Introduction

Words in our language can be split into categories that are helpful for teaching spelling. In this activity, the words we chose to focus on are words commonly referred to as sight words. These words are non-phonetic, which means they do not follow the concept that they can be sounded out. These words usually are the exceptions in our language and it is therefore easier to teach children to memorize them. For some children, this task can be difficult as it requires sequencing and working memory. This activity gives them additional practice in the spelling of these words in a fun and competitive way.

Good for...

Children who need extra practice reading and spelling non-phonetic sight words. Children who have sequencing challenges or low working memory as the amount of repetition will help them solidify and recall these words. The beauty of this activity is that it uses multiple pathways for learning and strengthens the recall of these words when using different learning modalities.

Time frame

10–15 minutes for playing. This exercise is best used every couple of days for those children who struggle with spelling these words. It can be integrated as part of an evening schedule of extra homework. The time is dependent on each child and how much they struggle with this particular type of learning.

Preparation/Materials

- 20 craft sticks
- A fine-point red pen
- A coffee mug
- A timer (for example, on a phone)
- Different tactile materials to trace on (e.g. something soft, something rough, smooth, bubbly). Alternatively, you can just use one plate each of a preferred tactile: sand, salt, flour – whatever your child's preference

Teaching tip

Kids love this game! Although it is about spelling, they love the fact that they can be successful and love to see you draw the 'Oops!' stick. In fact, you can use this technique for anything that needs to be memorized – maths facts, weekly spelling words for school and so on. Vary the tactile materials you offer or add another element to the game such as changing your voice for each spelling if kids feel reluctant to spell out loud.

Activity

This activity works best with a word bank of at least eight to ten non-phonetic words. You will need to write each word a minimum of three times to ensure multiple exposure to the word. On the craft sticks, write in red the word that your child struggles with. For example, if they struggle with the word 'of' then write this word on at least three craft sticks. You need to have at least eight to ten words you would like to practise. Once you have written each word three times on separate sticks, reserve six or seven craft sticks and write the word 'Oops!' on them. These sticks will be the sticks you use to restart the game. Once you have created all the sticks, place them word side down in a coffee mug so that players cannot see what word they are drawing. Before starting the game, set a time limit or limit of sticks a person must have to win the game. Taking turns, each player draws a stick from the mug, reads the word, then calls the word out loud, saying each letter while tracing it on the tactile surface they have chosen. Once they have successfully traced it, they retain the stick as part of their score. A player wins when they have the most sticks or the timer has gone off. If a player draws an 'Oops!' stick, they must put back all of their sticks and start the game again. It's important to stress to each player that they must both READ the name and say the word OUT LOUD as they trace it on the tactile surface. The saying and tracing ensures that the word is processed using two different modalities and aids in the retention of the word.

Follow-up
Make sure to follow up this game with the actual spelling of the word as part of a different spelling exercise. A student with dyslexia requires multiple exposure and practice in order to consolidate these words.

Word toolbox
The new words learned will depend on what the child has recently learned and what they need to practise. This game can be tailored to their individual needs and used regularly as part of their practice in order to help with this particular type of spelling.

4. Tap that Sound

Introduction
This activity is useful for phoneme segmentation (the ability to break words down into individual sounds), which is critical for accurate spelling as you need to hear the sounds to be able to spell accurately.

Good for...
Young children and beginning readers.

Time frame
This should take around one hour.

Teaching tip

Take your time with this – it is easy to make this a fun game.

Activity

Give your child a word – any word at all – and ask them to tap out the sounds they hear. Remember it is the sounds not the syllables. They can tap different objects in the room for every sound they hear, or tap a different part of their body.

Try to give them 10 words but vary the difficulty. For example, the word 'glad' has four sounds g/l/a/d/.

Easy words	Medium words	Difficult words
tip	dish	crash
map	flag	draft
box	gust	stamp
zip	ship	round
mud	strum	crest
sun	plush	shoulder

Follow-up

You can do this activity at the same time your child is reading with you. You can stop periodically and get them to practise this.

Learning chart

Prompt your child to record their learning.

Today I learned _____

Additional resources

www.scholastic.com/parents/books-and-reading/reading-resources/developing-reading-skills/teach-phonics-home.html

5. Rainbow Reading

Introduction

Reading for information can sometimes be a daunting task for students, and this may be particularly true for our dyslexic students who are then required to write a brief summary of what a chapter or a paragraph is about. When they are engaged in this type of reading, it is most useful to have some strategies that visually help them to remember what type of information they have just read and how to classify it accordingly. Rainbow reading encourages students to take notes as they read so that when they are finished they can easily sort through information and contextualize a passage.

Good for...

Secondary students or university students for learning how to take notes or study for tests/ exams. Ages 3–20.

Time frame

Dependent on how long it takes to read a passage or chapter.

Preparation/Materials

A package of different colour highlighters, ideally six different colours, and any reading passage.

Teaching tip

Students will need more practice with this technique at the beginning of their learning, but as time goes on it will become much easier. Start with paragraphs and work with your child if you can, and then move to more complex reading and allow them to take the lead.

Activity

Before embarking on a reading passage, assign a different open question for each colour of highlighter found in the package. For example, blue may represent any important people in relation to the reading. It answers the who question. Yellow may then answer the when question or deal with the time aspect. Each colour should represent a concept and be used accordingly while reading and taking notes. If a student encounters important people they will then highlight this information with the appropriate colour. By doing this, as the student reads, it helps to save time and visually identify the importance of a sentence to the paragraph or chapter. At the end of a chapter or pages, the student can easily make notes by going back and using the colours to take study notes or facts for a paper.

Follow-up
Websites for studying and note-taking strategies for dyslexic students.

Additional resources

www.readwritethink.org/classroom-resources/student-interactives
https://advice.writing.utoronto.ca/researching/summarize
https://justaddstudents.com/5-ways-to-teach-summarizing-skills

6. In Your Own Words

Introduction
The skill of paraphrasing is an invaluable tool for all students to learn. This is especially true of secondary school and university students who are required to write essays and take exams. This skill is one that takes attention and practice as it really is more than just paraphrasing – it is attending to what is most meaningful in a piece of writing, pulling out valuable information, and then using your own vocabulary and style to reiterate an idea. This is also an excellent technique to develop for study skills as it may contribute to overall comprehension of a piece and help with remembering crucial information.

Good for...
Reading comprehension, note taking, summarizing, study skills, essay and exam writing. Most suitable for young people aged 10–19.

Time frame
10–20 minutes, dependant on the length of the reading passage or chapter. This activity takes time to develop, so if this is a helpful goal in your child's learning, don't be afraid to spend up to three months mastering this skill until they can demonstrate a certain degree of proficiency in it.

Preparation/Materials
A piece of reading, note paper, highlighters.

Teaching tip

This skill can take a while to develop but it is a worthwhile skill to develop from an appropriate age. This is an activity that will take months to master, so be sure to keep it in the list of study skills to master.

Activity

While reading a piece, have the student highlight all the important information in a passage. This can be dates, ideas, people or experts – anything they think is important to the overall meaning of the passage. Once they feel they have everything highlighted, they can set about using their own words to summarize and reframe the passage. This process works best if they start with smaller pieces such as a paragraph or even a couple of sentences when they are first starting out. Once they have mastered a small amount, they move on to a larger piece of text until they can successfully do larger pieces of writing or even a chapter.

Follow-up

Search YouTube for examples of how to paraphrase and not plagiarize and then practise one new paragraph a week together until you feel your child has improved in this area.

Word toolbox

What words did your child learn today?

Additional resources

https://minds-in-bloom.com/teaching-kids-to-paraphrase-step-by-step
https://busyteacher.org/11272-how-to-teach-paraphrase-skills-pre-university.html

7. Family Newsletter

Introduction

This is an inclusive activity that can bring all members of the family together and help children brainstorm and generate ideas, practise their writing skills and get their creative juices flowing. The goals of this activity are to encourage children to practise their writing skills but also their ability to gather and research information on a basic level.

Good for...

Children who are comfortable with reading and writing. Younger children can work with older siblings on this activity and can contribute with pictures and drawings.

Time frame

This activity is best spread out over a week or so. This will allow the child or children to map out what important events and newsworthy family stories they will include in the newsletter and then draft out the parts. It will also allow time for children to prepare drawings and pictures to include in the newsletter.

Preparation/Materials

- Pictures, photos and drawings to be included in the newsletter
- Computer or laptop or paper if children want to create a hand-drawn newsletter
- Pens, pencils, crayons, felt markers, pencil crayons, paper

Teaching tip

This can be a bigger project for children but it can also be an exciting one. It would be good for you to help your child map out the highlights and distinguish between events that may be of interest to readers and ones that may not be ideal to include in the newsletter. This is project that can open up a good deal of dialogue between parents and children and can get them excited about sharing their family's news with others.

Activity

The following is a step-by-step process for this activity from beginning to end:

1. Brainstorm with your child the most recent events, activities, news items and interesting facts about your family. Help your child distinguish between items of interest versus items that may not be as exciting for others to hear about.
2. Study a newspaper with your child to get a feel for how a newspaper looks and what is included.
3. Decide how many items you will include in your newsletter.
4. Assign each item to a different member of the family, or your child can choose to take on all of them.
5. Encourage your child to think about their assigned topic/event using the five Ws (who, what, where, when, why).
6. For each assigned item, the assigned person can find photos of the event or draw pictures.

7. The assigned person can then begin outlining the details of the activity. This can be done as a brainstorm activity or in point form as an outline.

8. Once they have an outline, they can then begin describing the activity based on the outline or brainstorm.

9. Once everyone has completed their assigned activity or your child has completed all of their 'stories', these can be compiled in a newsletter format on the computer or on paper.

10. Send out the Family Newsletter to anyone to share your family's news!

Follow-up

For children who struggle with writing skills, help them or enable them to use speech-to-text programs to write down their thoughts. For younger children who want to be involved, help them by scribing their thoughts for them.

Challenge your child to expand their vocabulary by including interesting words and looking up synonyms for common words (e.g. instead of 'said', try using 'exclaimed' or 'shouted').

Word toolbox

Are there any new words that your child learned during the process of creating the newsletter? Did they learn to spell some new words? If so, did anything surprise them about the word's spelling or meaning?

Additional resources/ideas

Add some fun extras to your newsletter. Include a comic strip! This could be hand drawn or created on the computer. Include a jokes section and encourage your child to come up with some funny jokes. Has your family seen a movie recently? Include a movie review and rate it using their own rating scale.

Create your own crossword puzzle using this link: www.abcya.com/games/crossword_puzzle_maker

8. Story Sticks

Introduction

Story sticks are a great multisensory way to help your child develop reading comprehension. Having a jar of story sticks close by when you read with your child will give you an opportunity to check how well your child has comprehended what they have just read and also to help them reflect and think about it.

Good for...

Children of all ages. Story sticks can be used even if your child isn't reading independently yet. You can read a story to your child and use story sticks to ask them about the story they've just read or heard.

Time frame

The preparation time for this activity is the bulk of the time required. Once the story sticks themselves have been created, you can use them again and again any time your child reads a story or you read a story to them.

Preparation/Materials

- 10–15 craft sticks
- Permanent felt markers
- A list of comprehension questions/discussion topics
- A glass jar
- Printed out label (see the Appendix) to stick to your story sticks jar

Teaching tip

Before beginning a story, encourage your child to make predictions about the story while looking at the title, the front cover and the back cover. This will encourage them to begin thinking about what they're reading.

Activity

Using 10–15 craft sticks and your own comprehension questions or the comprehension question examples included in this activity, write one question on each stick and put them in a glass jar. Once your child has finished reading the story or book or you have finished reading the story to them, have your child pull out a story stick. If they are able, they can read the question or you can read the question and begin a discussion. Feel free to pick as many story sticks as you like to continue discussions about the story and to encourage your child to explore and reflect on their reading.

Example comprehension questions

1. Could this story be true? Why or why not?
2. Where does this story take place?
3. Who or what is this story about? Tell me more about them.
4. Does the main character have a problem? How is it solved?
5. What is the funniest, scariest or most interesting thing about this story?
6. Did anything happen in this story that has happened to you? Tell me about it.
7. Why do you think the author chose the title? How does it relate to the story?
8. If you could have a conversation with one of the characters, what would you say?
9. What changes might you make to the story?
10. Create a new ending for the story.
11. How does this story make you feel?
12. What message do you think the author wanted you to get?
13. Tell me what happened in the story.
14. What was the most important part of the story?
15. Would you recommend this story to a friend? Why or why not?

Follow-up

You can further the discussion with your child after reading stories by asking them what they still want to know. Use questions like, 'What questions do you still have about this story or book?' or 'What would you like to know more about?'

Word toolbox

Any time your child comes across a word they don't know, embark on a word discovery expedition and learn more about the word. Find the word's meaning but also try learning more about the word's origins by visiting Etymology Online: www.etymonline.com

Additional resources/ideas

To make comprehension and the learning even richer, begin a word web on the wall of your home. When you encounter words or phrases that spark curiosity or questions, write them on your word web and let that be a reminder to explore them more throughout the week.

9. Fortune Tellers

Introduction

This is a timeless and multisensory way to build reading review into your child's world. It's an engaging activity that has the additional aspect of folding paper to create a three-dimensional game.

Good for...

Children aged seven to adult. Depending on the child, the fortune tellers are generally easy to create. Younger children may need some help with the folding, but using the included worksheet and instructions (see the Appendix), it should be fairly easy for them to build a fortune teller with you.

Time frame

15–20 minutes to fold and build the fortune teller. Unlimited time to read what you have printed on the fortune teller.

Preparation/Materials

- Regular paper or origami paper
- Felt markers
- A list of words, phrases or sentences for your child to review
- The fortune teller worksheet (see the Appendix)

Teaching tip

You can use this activity to help your child review all kinds of concepts, including spelling lists that they bring home from school, words that you have encountered during story readings, or words that your child is struggling with. This is also a great activity for 'sight words' or high-frequency words that you want to encourage your child to learn and know by heart.

Activity

Print out the Fortune Teller worksheet. Make the fortune teller following the instructions. There are several options that you can write on the fortune teller. You can write the words that you want the child to review on the outside or inside. You can add phrases or sentences as well on the inside. The possibilities are endless!

Pick one of the top boxes (you can put colours on each box). Spell out the letters of that colour while alternating a pinching and pulling motion with the teller to reveal a set of four words. Pick a word and move the fortune teller the corresponding number of letters, revealing a second set of four words. Choose a flap to open and reveal your fortune!

Follow-up

Fortune tellers can be used for endless review of reading concepts. If your child is reviewing sounds for phonics, you can include sounds for review. For phonological awareness and for younger children who aren't reading yet, you can include pictures and have them name the picture and the beginning, middle or final sounds.

10. Skim, Scan, Yes You Can!

Introduction

When a reading difficulty persists, children can become easily disheartened and give up. This can happen particularly in secondary school and that might be the ideal time to teach them how to skim and scan for meaning. At that stage, reading for meaning can be the most important aspect. Skimming can help learners read more fluently as only the important parts of the text are read, and scanning can help the learner find the parts of the text they require. These are useful skills to master, particularly for further up the school and for university.

Good for...

Children who have difficulties with reading fluency and may stumble over small words and lose fluency as a result. It is good for studying a topic that has a heavy reading load.

Time frame

Allow one hour for this activity and make time the following week to practise what they have done in the activity.

Preparation/Materials

Select some passages from school readers or subject texts for the following week.

Teaching tip

This activity needs a lot of practice and it is a good idea to use a range of different texts of different degrees of difficulty.

Activity

As an example, children need to:

- skim the passage below as that will give them a background (sometimes called a schema) as to what it is about. They should try to read this quickly
- scan read the passage but beforehand note some questions they want to find the answers to.

An example of skimming and scanning using the first paragraph is shown after the passage.

What can we learn from the Spanish Flu 1918?

It is now over 100 years since the Spanish Flu struck the world with a vengeance. Following on closely from the end of World War I, it is estimated that the Spanish Flu resulted in more fatalities than the war. It is believed it was the most deadly pandemic in history and infected 500 million people worldwide. Unlike today, there was no computer analysis to record the number of victims of the Spanish Flu but it is believed that there were between 20 million and 50 million fatalities.

The world was taken by surprise by this pandemic. In fact, there is seldom any warning of a pandemic – it usually strikes fast and hard. As we know from the COVID-19 pandemic, any flu virus is highly contagious and can spread very quickly. When an infected person coughs or sneezes or even talks, respiratory droplets can be transmitted into the air, and these can be inhaled by people close by. A person can become infected if they touch something with the virus on it and then touch their mouth, eyes or nose. Young children, people over age 65, pregnant women and people with certain medical conditions, such as asthma, were most at risk. But the 1918 Spanish Flu struck down many previously healthy young people – a group normally resistant to this type of infectious illness. Just like the precautions taken for COVID-19, people in 1918 were ordered to wear masks, and schools, theatres and businesses were closed. It is unknown exactly where the particular strain of influenza that caused the pandemic came from but the 1918 flu was first seen in Europe, America and areas of Asia before spreading to almost every other part of the world within months.

Despite the fact that the 1918 flu was felt worldwide, it became known as the Spanish Flu, as Spain was hit hard by the disease and was not subject to the wartime news blackouts that affected other European countries. Because Spanish news sources were the only ones reporting on the flu, many believed it originated there (the Spanish, meanwhile, believed the virus came from France and called it the 'French Flu'). World War I had left parts of Europe and America with a shortage of doctors and other health workers, and hospitals in some areas were so overloaded with flu patients that schools, private homes and other buildings had to be converted into makeshift hospitals, some of which were staffed by medical students. By the summer of 1919, the pandemic had come to an end, as those that were infected had either died or developed immunity. Almost 90 years later, in 2008, researchers announced they'd discovered what made the 1918 flu so deadly: a group of three genes enabled the virus to weaken a victim's bronchial tubes and lungs and clear the way for bacterial pneumonia. Since 1918, there have been several other influenza pandemics – the 1957/58 flu epidemic; the H1N1 (or 'Swine Flu') pandemic of 2009/10; and, of course, the novel coronavirus pandemic of 2020 which has seen countries racing to find a cure for COVID-19.

Example of skimming

It is now over **100 years** since the **Spanish Flu** struck the world with a vengeance. Following on closely from the **end of World War I**, it is estimated that the Spanish Flu resulted in **more fatalities than the war**. It is believed it was the most deadly pandemic in history and **infected 500 million people worldwide**. Unlike today, there was **no computer analysis to record the number of victims of the Spanish Flu** but it is believed that there were between **20 million and 50 million fatalities**.

The words in bold are the key words and these words alone will provide you with the 'gist' of the passage. You can now do this with the whole passage.

Example of scanning

From this first paragraph I want to find out:

1. When did it happen?
2. What was it?
3. What were the consequences?

It is now over **100 years** since the **Spanish Flu** struck the world with a vengeance. Following on closely from the **end of World War I**, it is estimated that the Spanish Flu resulted in **more fatalities than the war**. It is believed it was the most deadly pandemic in history and **infected 500 million people worldwide**. Unlike today, there was **no computer analysis to record the number of victims of the Spanish Flu** but it is believed that there were between **20 million and 50 million fatalities**.

Now generate questions for the rest of the passage and practise scanning to get answers. The words in bold are the words that will provide you with the answers to your questions on the passage.

Follow-up

Investigate the Spanish Flu of 1918–20 and try to answer the question: What can we learn from this?

Word toolbox

Make a list of new words learned – to start with, put down the following: vengeance, analysis, respiratory, transmitted, resistance, bronchial.

Learning chart

Prompt your child to record their learning.

Today I learned _____

Additional resources

www.rms.com/blog/2018/04/20/reimagining-the-1918-pandemic?gclid=CjwKCAjw8MD7BRArEiwA GZsrBa5tKuB5kN9mu8Od_pMbhIPsw5fEmSg5Ew9ulCNczRCUik vVV6X0gRoCHaoQAvD_BwE

www.history.com/topics/world-war-i/1918-flu-pandemic

www.cdc.gov/flu/pandemic-resources/1918-pandemic-h1n1.html

www.nationalgeographic.com/history/2020/03/how-cities-flattened-curve-1918-spanish-flu-pandemic-coronavirus

11. Inferences: Reading Between the Lines

Introduction

It is not unusual for children with dyslexia to take the text they are reading literally. This may be because they are focusing on the decoding element of the reading process and less on the comprehension. Additionally, it is sometimes more difficult to detect the inferences made by the author if they are not clear in the text. Practice at inferential reading is important for children and young people with dyslexia and this is the aim of this activity.

Good for...

Establishing a routine of practising inferential reading and understanding and recognizing inferences.

Time frame

Around one hour.

Preparation/Materials

The factors that can help the reader identify the inference include:

- Background knowledge.
- Reading the text accurately.
- Being able to ask themselves questions such as: Does this make sense? Is there another way to look at this?
- Being able to look for clues in the text, such as key words, for example 'smirked', which give you a clue about the person, or 'cautiously', which also tells you something about the person.

Teaching tip

It might be a good idea to start with a practical activity such as a song but with some lines missing and they have to infer what these lines might be or how the singer may be feeling during the song.

Activity

Make up some situations that can occur in everyday life, for example, 'The boy banged the table when he was told he would miss the game' or 'The girl said to her mum I am not hungry when she was told the sushi was for dinner tonight.' What can you detect/infer from these?

Below are some situations. Ask your child to make up sentences either orally or written to include inferences about each situation.

For example:
We're having a birthday party in the back garden.

So, the child would say 'party hats', 'candles', 'presents' and 'birthday music'. These would be the inferences.

Now try these:
Her team just lost at a football game.

Inferences

_____

_____

_____

The dog excitedly jumped up to the lady as she put her hand in her pocket and took a small bag out.

Inferences

_____

_____

_____

The salesman said he would reduce the sofa by 75 per cent if you could take it away now.

Inferences

_____

_____

_____

The teacher shook her head at the children and said, 'Sorry, it is raining today.'

Inferences

_____

_____

_____

Follow-up

Your child could make facial expressions with friends and they have to guess the inference from that, for example the inference might be sad, tired etc.

Word toolbox

What words did your child learn today? Start with inference, excitedly, 75 per cent.

Learning chart

Prompt your child to record their learning.

Today I learned _____

Additional resources

https://examples.yourdictionary.com/examples-of-inference.html
www.youtube.com/watch?v=INFWXZ_tl4M

12. Say What You Mean: Rephrasing Challenging Passages

Introduction

Reading comprehension can be challenging for the young person with dyslexia, particularly if the passage is complex and elaborate vocabulary is used. Practice at reinterpreting passages into their own words can be very useful and it also helps them extend their vocabulary.

Good for...

Developing and extending vocabulary, summarizing information and developing confidence at tackling complex comprehension passages.

Time frame

Best not to rush this activity. Allow opportunities to revisit it.

Preparation/Materials

You can select passages from the internet. Book reviews can also be a good source of information and these can also be reinterpreted.

Teaching tip

It might be an idea to start by giving your child the meanings of some of the words to make the task less daunting. You will also need to read the quote to them – get them to read it with you or after you and tape them reading it!

Activity

We know that politicians at each end of the political spectrum often argue with each other – you might say always, not often. In historical terms, this is not new. One of the most famous in history was the rivalry between Benjamin Disraeli and William Gladstone in the 19th century. This is a well-known quote attributed to Disraeli when he was speaking about Gladstone: 'A sophistical rhetorician, inebriated with the exuberance of his own verbosity, and gifted with an egotistical imagination that can at all times command an interminable and inconsistent series of arguments to malign an opponent and to glorify himself.' Now there is a challenge for you.

The task is to put this quote in simple terms.

Your child can begin by looking up the meaning of each word, making two columns – the word and the meaning.

Then they can rewrite the quote so that they and their peer group at school can understand this.

Follow-up

As a follow-up, the child can write a reply to from Gladstone to Disraeli – using simple words!

They could also investigate using the internet to find other rivals – for example, political rivals or sports rivals – and make up a conversation between them!

Word toolbox

What words did your child learn today?

Learning chart

Prompt your child to record their learning.

Today I learned _____

Additional resources

https://artdiamondblog.com/archives/2008/12/inebriated_with.html

CHAPTER 3

Writing

We are sure that as parents, carers or teachers you can become quite frustrated and puzzled by the challenges some children with dyslexia have in putting pen to paper – particularly as they may be extremely competent orally and even have a rich vocabulary. It is also extremely frustrating for the child and this difficulty can lead to work avoidance and worse! When children are at this stage and having significant difficulties with writing, it is important to narrow down the task and break it into manageable chunks. It is important that they do not feel overwhelmed. Taking small steps is the key and this can lead to bigger and more significant steps.

We find games an effective way to help children develop writing skills. We have tried to make the games and activities in this chapter exciting and relevant. Our aim is to help the child achieve and particularly to break down the barriers that are preventing them from developing their writing skills to a higher level. Using technology is also useful and we have included some websites that may give you more ideas to help your child. We are fortunate that computers and laptops are readily available in schools but it is important that the child has the confidence to take risks with learning and with the writing process. We are hoping these activities will provide your child with some confidence and practice in writing that can make success in writing a reality.

ACTIVITIES

13. Sentence Roll

Introduction

This activity is great for children to expand their knowledge of the different parts of speech and their vocabulary and sentence-crafting skills. It's a great activity that can be played with parents and children alike.

Good for...

Children aged eight and up. Your child should be able to read and write.

Time frame

10–15 minutes.

Preparation/Materials

- Pens or pencils (can be coloured for extra fun)
- Printouts of the two Sentence Roll worksheets (see the Appendix)
- A set of four dice

Teaching tip

It's important for your child to be familiar with the basic grammar concepts included in the worksheets (nouns, verbs, adjectives). Review these with your child to help them understand what types of words these are.

Activity

Print out one copy of the 'Roll Out a Sentence!' worksheet. Print out copies of the second worksheet for each person playing. Each word on the first worksheet is assigned a number on the dice. The players take turns rolling all four dice to see what combination of numbers and words they will get. Once they have rolled, they fill out their words at the top of the sheet and then they create a sentence using those words. The fun part is seeing what kinds of silly sentence combinations each player ends up with.

Follow-up

To make this activity more engaging and interactive, players can draw pictures of their silly sentences.

Word toolbox

If you come across unfamiliar words in this activity, take some time to review these words with your child. Practise spelling them by tracing them on different surfaces around the house. Look up the words in the dictionary or online to get their definitions.

Additional resources/ideas

This activity can be extended by creating your own words and adding them to the mix.

Laminating the sheets or putting them in page protectors and writing on them using dry-erase markers will help make this activity last longer.

14. List It!

Introduction

Children with dyslexia often have difficulty generating ideas for writing. This activity gives them practice at coming up with ideas quickly and generates vocabulary. It also helps develop different types of thinking – literal, numeric, creative, word finding.

Good for...

Developing writing skills, and older students.

Time frame

20 minutes for two players. 10–15 minutes for more than two.

Preparation/Materials

- Dice/die
- Markers
- Game board (see the Appendix)

Teaching tip
This activity can take a bit of time so allow time and opportunities to make it a fun activity.

Activity
Use the game board (in the Appendix) or make your own board with the children. Each player takes a turn to roll the die and move the number of squares indicated. When they land on a square, they list orally all of the items they can name for that topic.

Follow-up
They can practise listing items for different topics, such as sport, a day in school, the weekend.

Additional resources
For older children: https://blog.reedsy.com/short-story-ideas

Helping young children to write a story: www.colorincolorado.org/article/helping-young-children-develop-strong-writing-skills

15. Story in a Bag

Introduction
Everyone needs a little encouragement to write. Many children with dyslexia feel overwhelmed by the writing process because of the level of difficulty required to write a piece. In order to engage a reluctant writer, it's always good to find ways to make writing fun. This activity can take away some of the reluctance of writing and provide a start to the writing process.

Good for...
Students aged 7–12 years who are reluctant writers.

Time frame
This activity could take a couple of hours or a couple of days depending on how reluctant your young writer is.

Preparation/Materials

A zip-lock bag with lots of cut-outs taken from magazines and newspapers. The bag must contain enough words and visual images for writers to create a story. Ensure you have enough pictures for your child to create characters and interesting words to use in their stories. When creating a story in a bag, aim for at least 20–25 pieces in the bag, consisting of approximately 10–12 pictures and 8–10 words.

Teaching tip

Take the time once you have explored all of the elements in the bag to orally develop the story and flesh out the ideas before you start. Take care to plan it somewhat by developing the plot and problem and use language like first, middle, end to provide some sort of structure for your child to work with. Write out a first draft and then once you are happy with the sequencing, your child can add their images and words to the final draft to celebrate their final story.

Activity

Once the bag has been prepared, tell your child that you will be creating a story together. Present the bag and tell them that they are supposed to create a story based on the images and words they find in the bag, and that you can help them with the process. For example, they can tell you the story and you can write it out for them. You can then use the images and cut-outs in the story and then you can write it together.

Follow-up

Brainstorm how to create and organize stories.

Additional resources

https://writeshop.com/plan-story-writing-kids

16. Noun and Verb Charades

Introduction

Charades is a timeless game that everyone can play. Incorporating learning within charades can be a win-win for parents and children! When thinking about writing and grammar, charades is a great way to reinforce the concept of nouns and verbs with your child.

Good for...

Children aged six to eight or any child who needs to be explicitly taught the concept of nouns and verbs and who may be struggling with solidifying this concept. The child should be able to read.

Time frame

15–20 minutes to prepare the cards. No preparation time to play the game.

Preparation/Materials

- A printout of the cards on sturdy cardstock (see the Appendix)
- Scissors
- Laminator (optional)

Teaching tip

Before beginning this activity, review with your child the definitions of nouns and verbs. Activate their knowledge in these two areas by asking eliciting questions such as, 'Point to three nouns in the room' or 'Tell me what the verb is in this sentence: I jumped on the trampoline.'

Activity

Print a copy of the cards provided onto sturdy cardstock. You can choose to laminate these cards if you have access to a laminator. Laminating helps the cards last longer. Cut out the individual cards and have them in a pile in-between you and your child. You can use the cards over and over again to solidify the concept of nouns and verbs or to just use them as a fun game!

Charades is a game that involves acting out words or phrases. In this case, you'll be acting out nouns or verbs. The object is to get your opponent to guess the answers using gestures alone. The one doing the acting out is not allowed to speak. The player acts out the word on the card and the other player tries to guess the correct word.

Follow-up

As an extension to this game, you could have a player pull a noun and a verb card together and act out both. To make the game a little more intense and competitive, you can time your rounds using a stopwatch. The words provided are generally at a basic level but should your child have difficulty reading the words, an image has been provided beside the word.

Word toolbox

If there are any words that your child doesn't know, engage in a conversation about that word and what that word might look like when you're acting it out.

17. Fun with Prepositions

Introduction

Prepositions are words that can describe place or location: on, over, below, above, under, at, for, in, off. Children with dyslexia often confuse these although they may well know the meaning of them.

Good for...

Most age groups but younger children will benefit from this activity as they are more inclined to make mistakes when describing the location of items using a preposition. Smaller children might enjoy physical demonstrations of what a preposition is – ask them to stand beside, in front, behind, on top of or under things around the house.

Time frame

It might be a good idea to carry out this activity every day for around a week. You can then test your child at the beginning of the following week.

Preparation/Materials

Have some pictures prepared that show the meaning of a preposition. Suggestions of prepositional phrases could be:

- behind the school
- on the desk
- under the bed
- down the drain
- in the toy cupboard
- above the shelf
- in front of the garden

Teaching tip

Try to make this as visual as possible by giving visual examples of the prepositions. Make it multisensory – you can give your child objects and ask them to put the objects under/above/in and so on, to show that prepositions are fully understood.

Activity

Make up different sentences using the prepositions from the list below.

Preposition	Sentence
with	
at	
from	
upon	
along	
across	
between	
down	
off	

Follow-up

Try to find other prepositions not included above and write sentences with them.

Word toolbox

What words did your child learn today? Try to include at least two new words.

Learning chart

Prompt your child to record their learning.

Today I learned _____

Additional resources

A fun activity with prepositions: https://learningspecialistmaterials.blogspot.com/2014/04/free-preposition-instruction-with.html

18. Running Family Story

Introduction

Keeping a running story going with your family can be a really fun and engaging way to encourage your child to tap into their imagination as well as practise their writing skills. There are virtually no limits to what stories you can create with family members!

Good for...

Children aged eight and up. Your child should be able to read and write.

Time frame

Five to ten minutes a day for as long as you want to keep it going.

Preparation/Materials

- Clipboard
- Paper
- Coloured pencils or pens

Teaching tip

Before beginning this activity, decide how long you will keep the running story going. You could choose a few days or up to a week or as long as you like, really. You can have the first person set the tone or the theme of the story by writing their first sentence or you can, as a family, decide on a theme or storyline and then go from there. Assign a colour to each person. That person will use their assigned colour every time they write their sentences.

Activity

The idea of this activity is to create a family story by having each family member craft one sentence at a time. Have the clipboard, paper and coloured pencils in one main area of the house. Flip a coin to see who will go first. The first person will begin the story by crafting the first sentence (e.g. It was a dark and stormy night when the lights went out and they heard a crash). The second person then writes their sentence continuing on with the story and so on, with all the participating members of the family. You can add to the story throughout the days or weeks. When the story feels as if it is finished or your time is up, sit down with the entire family and read the story together.

Follow-up

A wonderful extension activity can be to have your child or children draw pictures of parts of the story to make it come alive. Share the story with other family members or even in your Family Newsletter!

Word toolbox

If there are words that your child struggled with in spelling, this is a good opportunity to do some investigation about those words. Look them up in the dictionary with your child and have them review the meaning and the spelling by tracing them on several different tactile surfaces or writing them on a whiteboard in different colours.

19. Adjective Sensory Bag

Introduction

Learning to write colourfully and expressively is a talent and one that needs to be cultivated. Part of children achieving this skill is actively teaching them about the parts of speech that make up our language. This can include explicit teaching of terms such as nouns, verbs, adverbs and adjectives and highlighting what purpose they serve in our writing and why we need them. Teaching grammar doesn't have to be dry and boring; in fact, if you make it interesting it is more likely to be meaningful and successful!

Good for...

Teaching grammar structures and parts of speech, sentence writing, and crafting more colourful sentences.

Time frame

10–20 minutes.

Preparation/Materials

Three black bags with different objects in each of them:

- First bag – feel bag – contains items that feel smooth, bumpy, spiky, rough, round and so on.
- Second bag – sight bag – contains items that are colourful objects a child can see and describe as yellowish, round, big, small, red, purple and so on.
- Third bag – taste and smell bag – contains items that are sweet, sour, salty, fizzy, bitter; objects that smell, such as coffee grounds, an apple core, a ripe banana.

Teaching tip

Follow-up activities such as an adjective scavenger hunt, an adjective art gallery trip and adjective personality game will all act as a follow-up and reinforce the idea of what an adjective is. Afterwards, you can practise integrating them into written work.

Activity

The purpose of this activity is to include as many different items that feel, look, smell and taste so that your child can generate as many words as they can to describe them. Once they have successfully described them, you then explain that words used to describe how something looks, feels, tastes or smells are called adjectives. They describe things.

Follow-up

How to use adjectives in sentences to improve your writing. More practice with adjectives.

Additional resources

https://learningattheprimarypond.com/blog/5-fun-activities-for-teaching-adjectives-in-the-primary-grades

26. Character on Social Media

Introduction

This activity asks children to create a social media profile for a character in a book or short story. Based on evidence, facts and storyline, children can create what they think this character's social media profile would look like. This is a great way for children to bring the characters to life and to create more depth to their understanding of the character and the story.

Good for...

Children aged eight years and up. Children should be able to read and write.

Time frame

Five minutes to prepare and print off the worksheet (or longer if your child wants to draw their own worksheet). Unlimited time for your child to create the profile page.

Preparation/Materials

- Pen or pencil
- A printout of the worksheet (see the Appendix)
- Blank paper if your child wants to create their own page
- Coloured pencils or pens or felt pens to draw pictures

Teaching tip

Encourage your child to think about the 'voice' of the character based on what they have read in the novel or the story. What kinds of things might they say and *how* might they say them? This provides an opportunity for your child to really think about the character's personality, where they are from, their age and their background.

Activity

The idea of this activity is to encourage your child to dig deeper into characters in books they are reading and to begin to think critically about the characters. No matter who the character is or the time period of the book, a great way to make characters relatable to children is to imagine what their social media page might look like. What kinds of things might they post on their page? What are their interests? Who might be their friends (other characters in the book) and what might they post on their page? Children can draw pictures of 'photos' that the character might have on their page and their profile picture. This activity is a wonderful way to engage the child more in the book or novel they are reading.

Follow-up

Once your child has created the character's social media page, engage in a discussion and ask them about their choices. Enquire into their reasoning behind their decisions and talk about why they felt the character would post certain things on their page. There are no wrong answers here – just curiosity and more engagement in the story.

Word toolbox

What is social media? Take some time to look it up and discuss what the purpose is and how it has made our world better or worse.

Additional resources/ideas

This might be another opportunity for you and your child to engage in a discussion about social media itself and its pros and cons. What might the book's characters feel about social media?

21. Blog It!

Introduction

Help your child start their own blog or start a family blog together! There are so many benefits to this activity for kids. These include teaching your child about the internet and internet safety, practising writing for an audience, keyboarding practice, and motivation for writing practice on a platform other than paper and pen.

Good for...

Children aged eight and up. Your child should be able to read and write.

Time frame

Five to ten minutes a day for as long as you want to keep it going.

Preparation/Materials

- Computer/laptop/tablet with keyboard
- Internet access
- Photos, story ideas, pictures and so on

Teaching tip

While it can be easy to jump in to signing up and starting a blog, it's a good idea to sit down with your child and map out the blog. Discuss and write down things you want to talk about, photos you might want to share and what kinds of things you want to explore. It's also a good idea to talk to your child about internet safety, online ethics and being responsible on the internet. Some good websites to help you with these conversations are:

www.connectsafely.org/parentguides

https://mediasmarts.ca

www.commonsense.org/education/articles/23-great-lesson-plans-for-internet-safety

Tips for blog planning

Look for examples of strong blogs. Talk about what you like about these blogs and what you don't. Some good examples of sites to look at are:

http://onekidslife.com

http://theycallmet.com

http://kristinandkayla.blogspot.com

https://elliotmast.blogspot.com

Do some blog brainstorming. Brainstorm by answer the following questions:

1. What do you love to do in your spare time (think sports, hobbies, activities etc.)?
2. What are some things that you know a lot about? Write it all down (think about things like animals, crafts, books, cooking etc.).
3. How can you help other people or kids with your blog? What are some things that you can offer people who visit your blog?
4. Who will be your audience? Who do you want to read your blog?
5. Do you want to do the blog alone or do you want to share the writing duties with your siblings, parents or friends?

Activity

Once you have made your plan and had the important discussion about internet safety, you're ready to explore your blogging options. There are so many options out there but there are some that are specific to students and children. The links below are some to check out:

https://kidblog.org/home

https://education.weebly.com

https://edublogs.org

Follow-up

A great way to encourage collaboration is to have your child write a blog with a person or your whole family. This way, everyone can contribute something and everyone can collaborate and create a wonderful way to connect to others.

Word toolbox

If your student struggles with spelling, encourage them to write down words that are causing them problems and look them up together. Have a whiteboard near the computer so your child can jot down words they aren't sure about and discuss them later.

Additional resources/ideas

To delve deeper into blog planning, try out this free Student Blogging Unit plan: https://kidblog. org/home/free-blogging-lesson-plans. It's a great resource to help get you started!

22. Bizarre Beginnings and Crazy Endings

Introduction

Expressive writing can be problematic for young people with dyslexia – irrespective of their age. Usually children with dyslexia can have an excellent imagination and be quite creative. The problem is that often they are not able to show this in their written work. It is a good idea to foster their creativity and help them develop this in their writing. This can be a good step towards expressive writing that can justify their abilities. This activity provides an example of how this can be done and how the creativity and imagination of the child can be developed.

Good for...

Developing creativity, extending expressive writing, getting started on a piece of written work and having an interesting ending.

Time frame

Allow perhaps three 30-minute sessions for this.

Preparation/Materials

Comic books can be useful – looking at the crazy situations characters sometimes get themselves into.

Teaching tip

It might be an idea to help by brainstorming with your child and making a list of all the interesting and unusual or even ridiculous words you can think of.

Activity

You will find three suggestions below for bizarre beginnings and crazy endings. The child will have to fill in the gaps between the beginning and the ending.

Then they should make up their own story with bizarre beginnings and crazy endings.

Bizarre beginnings	????	Crazy endings
The dog lined up for the tickets for the hip hop rave…		Lying flat out, the dog gave a scream of delight.
The table shrieked when…		The two chairs wobbled with delight.
The elephant combed his trunk and…		….and chased his shadow.

Follow-up

Make a comic story line with drawings and speech bubbles using the examples shown above.

Word toolbox

What words did your child learn today? Start with rave, shrieked, delight, shadow, combed.

Learning chart

Prompt your child to record their learning.

Today I learned _____

Additional resources

www.vocabulary.com/lists/23400

23. Cut It Out! Success with Summaries

Introduction

Often children with dyslexia have difficulties summarizing information. They may have difficulty in identifying the key points and sequencing these points in a logical order. This activity provides practice at summarizing information.

Good for...

Extending vocabulary, summarizing information, reflective writing.

Time frame

This can be a lengthy task, so it may be useful to break it into different parts.

Preparation/Materials

Watch and listen to a football game and pay particular attention to the commentary. Discuss the commentary afterwards and the kinds of words used by the commentator.

Teaching tip

It might be an idea to have your child listen to a short extract from a radio football commentary to get the idea and flavour and particularly how the commentators sum up the action.

Activity

You will see below the second-half commentary of a football game between Tottenham Hotspur and West Ham United. The game was played on Sunday, 18 October 2020. It was clearly an exciting game as the half-time score was Tottenham Hotspur 3, West Ham United 0 – and as you can see from the second-half commentary, the game looked quite a bit different at full time.

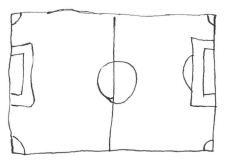

The activity is to write a summary of the second half, from 46 minutes to 96 minutes. Your child needs to consider:

- making it exciting for the reader
- making sure they have given a good account of the second half
- trying to avoid repeating the words in the commentary
- trying to capture the flavour, the score and the excitement in two paragraphs.

Words that might be used (but you do not have to):

astonishing	defensive	attacking
comeback	sensational	narrow
clincher	roar	celebration
caution	brutal	competitive

Commentary: Tottenham Hotspur v West Ham United

Second half begins, Tottenham Hotspur 3, West Ham United 0

46' Moussa Sissoko (Tottenham Hotspur) wins a free kick in the defensive half.

48' Attempt missed. Arthur Masuaku (West Ham United) left-footed shot from the left side of the box is high and wide to the right.

50' Attempt blocked. Michail Antonio (West Ham United) right-footed shot from the left side of the box is blocked. Assisted by Arthur Masuaku.

52' Attempt missed. Harry Kane (Tottenham Hotspur) left-footed shot from outside the box is too high.

53' Attempt missed. Pablo Fornals (West Ham United) header from very close range is just a bit too high.

55' Attempt blocked. Tomáš Souček (West Ham United) header from the centre of the box is blocked. Assisted by Jarrod Bowen with a cross.

61' Attempt saved. Harry Kane (Tottenham Hotspur) right-footed shot from outside the box is saved in the bottom left corner. Assisted by Pierre-Emile Højbjerg.

67' Attempt blocked. Harry Kane (Tottenham Hotspur) right-footed shot from the right side of the box is blocked. Assisted by Son Heung-min.

71' Substitution, Tottenham Hotspur. Harry Winks replaces Tanguy Ndombele.

72' Substitution, Tottenham Hotspur. Gareth Bale replaces Steven Bergwijn.

72' Angelo Ogbonna (West Ham United) is shown the yellow card for a bad foul.

75' Steven Bergwijn (Tottenham Hotspur) wins a free kick in the attacking half.

77' Substitution, West Ham United. Manuel Lanzini replaces Pablo Fornals.

77' Substitution, West Ham United. Andriy Yarmolenko replaces Michail Antonio.

80' Substitution, Tottenham Hotspur. Lucas Moura replaces Son Heung-min.

80' Offside, West Ham United. Arthur Masuaku tries a through ball, but Manuel Lanzini is caught offside.

82' Foul by Moussa Sissoko (Tottenham Hotspur).

82' Goal! Tottenham Hotspur 3, West Ham United 1. Fabián Balbuena (West Ham United) header from the centre of the box to the bottom right corner. Assisted by Aaron Cresswell with a cross following a set-piece situation.

85' Own goal by Davinson Sánchez (Tottenham Hotspur). Tottenham Hotspur 3, West Ham United 2.

89' Manuel Lanzini (West Ham United) wins a free kick in the attacking half.

89' Attempt blocked. Jarrod Bowen (West Ham United) left-footed shot from the left side of the box is blocked. Assisted by Aaron Cresswell with a cross.

89' Lucas Moura (Tottenham Hotspur) wins a free kick in the defensive half.

89' Arthur Masuaku (West Ham United) is shown the yellow card for a bad foul.

90' Foul by Harry Kane (Tottenham Hotspur).

90+2' Attempt missed. Gareth Bale (Tottenham Hotspur) left-footed shot from the centre of the box is close, but misses to the right. Assisted by Harry Kane following a fast break.

90+3' Robert Snodgrass (West Ham United) wins a free kick on the left wing.

90+3' Aaron Cresswell (West Ham United) wins a free kick in the defensive half.

90+3' Foul by Serge Aurier (Tottenham Hotspur).

90+4' Goal! Tottenham Hotspur 3, West Ham United 3. Manuel Lanzini (West Ham United) right-footed shot from outside the box to the bottom right corner following a set-piece situation.

90+5' Manuel Lanzini (West Ham United) is shown the yellow card for excessive celebration.

90+6' Second half ends, Tottenham Hotspur 3, West Ham United 3.

https://talksport.com/football/premier-league/match/2020–10-18/tottenham-hotspur-v-west-ham-united

https://www.theguardian.com/football/live/2020/oct/18/tottenham-hotspur-v-west-ham-united-premier-league-live

See also the YouTube summary: www.youtube.com/watch?v=3fRiCVS6wPY

Follow-up

Your child could make up their own commentary and summary for a school football game – they could do this with some friends, tape it and listen to it to work out how they might improve it. See: www.learnesl.net/how-to-write-commentary-script-for-football-match-with-example

Look at some other websites with some popular football phrase such as: '12 of the best football commentaries of all time'. See: https://bleacherreport.com/articles/1060662-12-of-the-best-goal-commentaries-of-all-time

Find out the meaning of the phrase 'pep talk' – the West Ham United Manager gave his players a pep talk at half time. What does this mean? Your child could make up their own pep talk to someone who is losing a game. What would they say?

Word toolbox

What words did your child learn today?

Learning chart

Prompt your child to record their learning.

Today I learned _____

Additional resources

Select two football commentators from this website and write a short biography about them:

https://en.wikipedia.org/wiki/List_of_British_football_commentators

24. Art Smarty: Seeing the Unseen

Introduction

There is usually a great deal of emphasis on helping the child with dyslexia to develop reading skills – this is perfectly understandable. But this can sometimes be at the expense of developing their creativity and imagination. It can have a detrimental impact on creative writing. It is important that this does not happen and that every effort is made to harness and develop the child's imagination and creative skills.

Good for...

This activity aims to develop creativity and help the child utilize their imagination and use this effectively in creative writing. Suitable for any ages.

Time frame

This activity should not be rushed, so take as long as required.

Preparation/Materials

It is a good idea to prepare your child for this by getting them to listen to some meditative-type music, close their eyes and think of an image they like.

Teaching tip

The preparation is important – listening to music and relaxation is good preparation. You can also take any random picture and do a brainstorming with your child to encourage imaginative thinking.

Activity

For this activity, the child will need to look at the image of the children's playground and write a story about it – trying to use their imagination and not just write about what they can see but what they cannot see!

For example: who is supposed to be watching the kids? What do you think they are saying to each other? What kind of shops are nearby?

Follow-up

They can now do this with their own image – they should draw an image. It does not have to be artistic. It is an image and sometimes images only really make sense to the artist! Then they can make up a story about the image using their imagination – seeing the unseen.

Word toolbox

What words did your child learn today?

Learning chart

Prompt your child to record their learning.

Today I learned _____

Additional resources

https://thewritepractice.com/creative-writing-prompts

25. Patchwork Quilt

Introduction

We often find that children with dyslexia have difficulties in getting started with a writing piece. This applies to children of all ages. But once they get a start or they are provided with some cues, they are off! This exercise provides phrases that they can use and helps them also to think outside the box.

Good for...

Children and young people of all ages. It helps with creativity but also written expression.

Time frame

You could give them an hour to do this but it's best to break it up into chunks – depending on the age of the child.

Preparation/Materials

You can discuss the writing process with them and perhaps some of the vocabulary below.

Teaching tip

It is a good idea to discuss a possible story with your child first – as a follow-up they can insert their own words from a story they have previously written.

Activity

They need to write a story using as many of the words/phrases below as possible – they can put in some of their own phrases too.

As an option, you can give them a possible first sentence:

It was a warm night for November and everyone was excited at the celebrations that were planned.

surprise	crazy	as quick as a flash	he was trembling
shock	never again	never believe this	stranger
glad it is all over	police	friendly faces	lots of people
flashing light	expression	loud noise	full moon
fireworks	dancing to the music	embrace	shouting at the top of my voice

Follow-up

As a follow-up you can provide a blank patchwork quilt and ask them to fill in the spaces – with children's names, street names or the names of towns.

Word toolbox

Depending on the age of the child – the above is aimed at aged nine but younger and older children can use this. New words might include: trembling, expression, stranger, flashing.

Learning chart

Prompt your child to record their learning.

Today I learned _____

Additional resources

www.scholastic.com/teachers/articles/teaching-content/teaching-techniques-encouraging-expressive-writing

www.understood.org/en/learning-thinking-differences/child-learning-disabilities/writing-issues/6-skills-kids-need-for-written-expression

www.readandspell.com/how-to-improve-writing-skills-for-kids

CHAPTER 4

Spelling

Spelling can be very troublesome for children with dyslexia and it is worthwhile spending a great deal of time teaching spelling and working with spelling through games and activities. Spelling can have an impact on writing and although the learner may have a rich vocabulary, they may be reluctant to use that due to difficulties with spelling.

Spelling can be useful for understanding the rules and conventions of the English language and this can have a positive spin-off effect on reading.

The activities we have included here are mainly multisensory, and using all the modalities is a good and fun way to learn spelling. Spelling lends itself to games and everyone can join in and that makes it more of a family activity. The Spelling Art Wall activity, for example, requires a degree of creativity as well as working with others and can also be ideal for working at home! The activities can be accessed by children of all ages but some, such as the Sensory Spelling activity, are ideal for younger children.

It is also important to recap when learning spelling and we have included some tips for this as well as consolidation activities. It is a good idea to try to reverse any negative views the child may have of spelling, and the games and activities in this chapter attempt to do just that!

ACTIVITIES

26. Words within Words

Introduction

A fun and encouraging way to get kids interested in words is to create interesting activities or quizzes to get them thinking differently about what they see. This activity allows them to see smaller parts of words contained within larger words or to manipulate letters in order to spell different words. They are 'word detectives' searching for smaller units within something bigger. You can play this activity as a family or simply put a word challenge on your fridge and have them look at it as they pass through the kitchen. You can also put a copy on their bedroom door so that it catches their interest during the day.

Good for...

Kids of any age. Assists with mental manipulation of letters, and helps with sequencing, spelling and visual tracking.

Time frame

For games, you can assemble more words and make a game out of it or you can merely have it as an individual activity that gets completed throughout the day. Five to ten minutes a day.

Preparation/Materials

If you are doing it as a daily challenge, you can print it off on the computer and stick it to any high-traffic area throughout the house. If you have a whiteboard in the kitchen, or in their bedroom, you can use this as well. Make sure you have the tools readily available. Put a pen on a string next to the paper, so that everyone has what they need to write it down. Make it easy and they will rise to the challenge!

Teaching tip

Get the whole family interested. Have them track words on the sheet. Put the family into teams and see who can come up with the most words. Put words in their lunch box. Set up a speed challenge before dinner. Make it fun and interesting and your kids will learn to love words!

Activity

Find a fairly large word which contains many smaller word combinations inside it. The larger the word, the better. Have your children or family see how many words they can create with all of the letters contained in the first larger word. They can write them down or tell you. You can start the challenge by creating or finding words and writing them down so that people can add to it.

27. Sports Day Spelling

Introduction

Help your child review their spelling words or words that they continually struggle with by having a Sports Day Spelling! Incorporating movement and spelling can help make spelling multisensory and can also help your child solidify those words they need to remember.

Good for...

Children aged eight years and up. Your child should be able to read and write.

Time frame

20–30 minutes.

Preparation/Materials

- A list of spelling words for review
- A skipping rope
- Pavement chalk
- A bouncy ball

Teaching tip

While we have listed some general activities here, you can adjust this activity to include sports and activities that your child enjoys such as jumping on a trampoline or football.

Activity

Incorporating multisensory ways to review and reinforce concepts has proven to be effective for students of all abilities. Incorporating movement can be highly effective for children who are diagnosed with attention- or focus-related conditions or children who simply have a hard time staying still for long periods.

When you have chosen the activity or activities that you will be using and your list of words, set up an area either outside or a larger open area inside and set up sports 'stations' (e.g. a skipping rope station, a jumping jacks station, a ball bounce station). Assign a certain number of words to each station and have your child move through the stations doing the activity while spelling the words. Ensure your child is actually spelling the words correctly for effective review. You can create a reward for finishing the sports day such as a treat or screen time or anything that helps to positively reinforce the task that they completed.

Follow-up

If you have more than one child, you can have separate lists for each child at each station. You can have a small competition on who can complete the stations first and have prizes for first, second or third place.

28. Spelling Art Wall

Introduction

Students who struggle with reading, writing and especially spelling often want to avoid spelling practice at all costs. One way to make reviewing spelling fun and engaging is to create a Spelling Art Wall. This encourages spelling review *and* creativity all at the same time – the perfect combination.

Good for...

School-aged children who are able to read and write.

Time frame

Preparation time: 15–20 minutes. Time for review/drawing: endless!

Preparation/Materials

- A large roll of drawing paper or large posterboards
- All kinds of felt pens, coloured pencils, crayons, pencils, pens, coloured pens
- Glitter glue (optional)
- Poster paints (optional)

- Words to review with your child. Try to divide the words into phonetically regular words (words that you can sound out) and non-phonetic words (irregular words)

 ## Teaching tip

When reviewing phonetically spelled words, encourage your child to sound as they spell the words when they are spelling them on the wall. If you are having your child spell out non-phonetically spelled words or irregularly spelled words that cannot be sounded out, have them name the letters as they spell as this makes the task of spelling these words more of a sequencing activity rather than a spelling activity that allows them to rely on phonics.

Activity

Find some spare wall space in your home and tape up a large piece of drawing paper. Dictate a word to your child and have them spell the word on the paper in any size or shape. Be sure to have them sound the word out or name the letters as they spell. Once they have done that, encourage them to 'artify' the word by going over it with felt pens, coloured pencils, glitter glue or poster paint. Each time they go over the word, make sure to have them sound the word out or name the letters. Continue doing the same with the remainder of your words until you have filled the drawing paper with an art wall of spelling words.

Follow-up

Be careful! These art walls can become addictive and things that your child can become attached to and want to keep. If you find that your child is enjoying displaying their art wall, you can use this as an opportunity for them to review their words. Have them trace over the words with their fingers and sound the word out or name the letters as they do so.

 ## Word toolbox

If your child is unsure of the definition of a word, use this as an opportunity to look up the word in the dictionary together. You can have your child draw pictures around the word to encourage them to remember its meaning.

 # 29. Sensory Spelling

Introduction

This activity is perfect for any parent challenged by weekly spelling lists and how to make studying for them more interesting. Often, kids are expected to remember a list of 10–15 words per week, and for some students this can be a challenge. One strategy to use is overlearning so that a student has had enough practice.

Good for...

Younger students in primary years who need extra practice memorizing spelling lists or tricky non-phonetic words.

Time frame

Five to ten minutes each night before the weekly test so that children have had multiple attempts to overlearn the spelling list.

Preparation/Materials

Several baking trays with different tactile elements added to them. You can also use large surfaces with different textures to practise writing on. The aim of sensory spelling is to find as many different surfaces as possible that a student can use to practise their spelling words on. For example, you can have baking trays filled with sand, flour, beads, dry beans. You can also try zip-lock bags with different gels and squishy materials. You can add sparkles or whatever your child likes. For different tactile materials, think surfaces that are rough, smooth, bumpy, soft and so on. Fabric stores generally have a good selection of fabrics which fit the bill at a low cost.

Teaching tip

Try building a small selection at first to see what surfaces your child prefers. After that, try coming up with as many different tactile surfaces you can think of to try your spelling words on.

Activity

Starting at the beginning of the week, pick a new tactile surface to practise your weekly spelling words with. Try to use a different surface for each practice session, noting the ones that your child prefers. Typically, each word should be practised eight to ten times during the week in order for your child to secure the spelling. Take turns naming the letters and writing the word, saying the words out loud as they go. This way, different learning modalities are engaged and help to secure the new learning. For example, you will remember something more deeply if you trace and say it rather than just trace the letters. This is because different parts of your learning brain are engaged simultaneously and make learning easier.

Follow-up

Other multisensory tricks to use to study and learn.

30. Make Your Own Mnemonic

Introduction

If you have ever had trouble remembering and sequencing anything, you will most likely be familiar with the idea of a mnemonic. A mnemonic is a memory aid that you use to remember something tricky. For example, you may be familiar with this mnemonic: All Good Boys Deserve Fudge. This helps us to remember a major scale in music. Never Eat Shredded Wheat is another favourite for memorizing the points on a compass. You can use a mnemonic to help with all sorts of things on any subject area. Often children with dyslexia prefer to remember tricky facts, sequences or spellings by using a mnemonic.

Good for...

Spelling tests, history dates, science class, maths class – in fact, any class!

Time frame

10–15 minutes.

Preparation/Materials

A list of anything your child is having trouble memorizing. It could be a weekly spelling list, science class, geography class, history class.

Teaching tip

Mnemonics help everyone. If you are having difficulty creating your own, take a look online for some easier ones and this may help you or inspire you to create your own. If you can't create your own, you may want to borrow something you like and practise using it.

Activity

Pinpoint an area where your child is having trouble remembering or sequencing something and figure out how you can incorporate a mnemonic to help. For example, if your child is having difficulty memorizing a spelling word, you need to create a catchy way to help. The word 'because' often causes a lot of trouble for primary school children because of the number of vowels in it. You can give them this sentence to help them remember the order of the letters as they appear in the word: Big Elephants Can Actually Understand Small Elephants. In this sequence, the first letter of each word corresponds with a letter found in the tricky word. What is most important about using mnemonics is that they are catchy and easy for a child to use. You can be creative in making your own mnemonics but be mindful to keep them simple. The purpose of this activity is remembering the sequencing of something so that your child can remember it. Set aside time to memorize the mnemonic and quiz each other. You could do this over breakfast, on the drive to school, as you get dressed in the morning – virtually anywhere.

Follow-up
As a follow-up try to make a mnemonic of a hobby or sport you play or a television programme or film you have seen recently.

Word toolbox
What words did your child learn today? Start with mnemonic, sequencing.

31. Spin It and Write It!

Introduction
Reviewing spelling can feel like an arduous task for parents and can often end up in frustration as this seems to sometimes be the last thing our children with learning challenges want to do. Turning spelling review into a game can make this task less arduous and, dare we say it, fun!

Good for...
School-aged children or any child who can read or write.

Time frame
Preparation time: approximately 10 minutes to prepare the board. Reviewing time: endless!

Preparation/Materials

- A printout of the provided worksheet (see the Appendix)
- A laminator or access to a laminator at your local print shop
- A dry-erase marker or a regular marker for non-laminated worksheets
- Brass paper fasteners for the spinner

You can also use an old spinner that has numbers from a board game that you have lying around.

Teaching tip

If your child is spelling words they can sound out (phonetically regular words), ask them to sound out as they spell. If they are reviewing non-phonetic or irregular words (words they can't sound out), have them name the letters as they spell.

Activity

Print out the provided worksheet on heavy cardstock. Ideally, this can be laminated so that you can reuse it over and over. Using a brass fastener, poke a hole in the middle of the spinner and attach an arrow or pointer to the middle of the spinner. You can also use a numbered spinner from any board game that you may have in your home. List your review words on the numbered spaces. Have your child spin the spinner and spell out the word in the spaces below. Make it more of a game by seeing which word gets spelled the most.

Follow-up

You can reuse this fun activity board any time your child comes home with spelling review words from school.

Word toolbox

Be sure to look up any word that your child is unsure about or doesn't know, and use that as an opportunity to explore the word's meaning and origins.

Additional resources/ideas

These are fun reusable spinners that you can have on hand for all kinds of activities like this:

www.amazon.ca/Learning-Advantage-7350-Transparent-Spinners/dp/B00M1HACVC

32. Rainbow Word Spelling

Introduction

Why not make reviewing spelling words with your child a little more imaginative, creative and fun? Spelling rainbow words can be just what makes this task easier to do with your child.

Good for...

School-aged children or any child who can read or write.

Time frame

Preparation time: less than five minutes. Activity time: endless!

Preparation/Materials

- A printout of the provided worksheet (see the Appendix)
- Regular paper or cardstock
- Different coloured felt pens or coloured pencils or crayons
- A laminator or access to a laminator (optional)
- A list of words for spelling review

Teaching tip

If your child is spelling words they can sound out (phonetically regular words), ask them to sound out as they spell. If they are reviewing non-phonetic or irregular words (words they can't sound out), have them name the letters as they spell.

Activity

Using your list of words, you can either dictate the words for your child and have them spell them on the spaces beside the rainbows, or you can put the words there yourself if you are simply wanting them to have repeated review of the words. Once your child has their list of words beside a rainbow, they can then write them in the different parts of the rainbow with different coloured pencils, crayons or pens.

Follow-up

You can reuse this fun activity board any time your child comes home with spelling review words from school.

Word toolbox

Be sure to look up any word that your child is unsure about or doesn't know and use that as an opportunity to explore the word's meaning and origins.

Additional resources/ideas

If you choose to laminate this activity, you can reuse it any time for different purposes. You can even use this for maths facts, vocabulary study words and more!

33. Spelling Sleuths

Introduction

Everyone loves a good mystery to solve. Have your child review their spelling words by becoming a spelling sleuth and creating their own secret code for their words.

Good for...

School-aged children or any child who can read or write.

Time frame

Five minutes to print out the worksheet provided. 15–20 minutes or more for the activity.

Preparation/Materials

- A printout of the worksheet (see the Appendix)
- Pencil or pen, crayons
- A list of spelling words for review

Teaching tip

If your child is spelling words they can sound out (phonetically regular words), ask them to sound them out as they spell. If they are reviewing non-phonetic or irregular words (words they can't sound out), have them name the letters as they spell.

Activity

Using your list of spelling words, have your child spell out the words and then you put the words into code using the Spelling Sleuths secret code provided. Your child then has to decode as many words as they can. You can offer them an additional challenge by setting a time limit on how long they can take to decode a word.

Follow-up

Reuse this fun activity board any time your child comes home with spelling review words from school.

Word toolbox

Be sure to look up any word that your child is unsure about or doesn't know, and use that as an opportunity to explore the word's meaning and origins.

Additional resources/ideas

Your child can use their Spelling Sleuths secret code to create their own secret messages. Help them write secret messages to their friends or other family members. Help them solve the message using the secret code on the worksheet.

34. Sounds the Same

Introduction

For many children with dyslexia, spelling can be a real barrier to writing. But they can overcome this by noting the sound of the word as well as the visual features of the word. When they come across what are known as homophones, spelling can be even more problematic.

Homophones are words that sound the same but are spelled differently such as 'to' and 'too'. They can also be spelled exactly the same but have different meanings like 'rose' and 'rose'. This exercise will help them practise spelling homophones.

Good for...

Children of all ages, particularly later stages of primary and early secondary school.

Time frame

You can spend an hour on this exercise and make up some similar follow-up materials.

Preparation/Materials

It is a good idea to discuss this with the learner and give some examples of homophones. You do not need to use the technical word 'homophones' but showing some examples will be necessary.

Teaching tip

It is a good idea to give a number of examples and try to get the child to do several before starting this exercise.

Activity

The child has to fill in the blanks in the passage below by choosing the correct word from this list.

weigh	fair	weight	too
hour	time	knight	cereal
week	serial	coarse	walk
idle	wait	so	break
course	brake	bare	way
bear	night	our	to
thyme	fare	weak	sow
wok	pore	pour	idol

Breakfast is always a morning rush. I _____ my juice _____ slowly and my brother shouts, 'I want _____ go to school on _____,' I think he can _____ as he knows the _____, The start of the week of _____ is always bad. But as well as my Dad, I _____ eat my _____ slowly as I do not have a _____ until later in the morning and I cannot _____ to be hungry. It is different late at _____, as I am okay at that _____ but the morning is my eating time!! I think that is _____ – at least I am not _____ and I sometimes _____ our dog.

Follow-up

You can ask children to make up a homophone song – they can get an idea from this YouTube video: www.youtube.com/watch?v=0dep8_ARiSU

Word toolbox

What words did your child learn today?

Additional resources

https://onlineteachersuk.com/english-homophones

Answers

> Breakfast is always a morning rush. I always pour my juice so slowly and my brother shouts, 'I want to go to school on time.' I think he can wait as he knows the way. The start of the week of course is always bad. But as well as my Dad, I too eat my cereal slowly as I do not have a break until later in the morning and I cannot bear to be hungry. It is different late at night, as I am okay at that hour but the morning is my eating time!! I think that is fair – at least I am not idle and I sometimes walk our dog.

35. Spelling Across the Curriculum: Subject-Specific Vocabulary

Introduction

As children progress further up the school some subject vocabulary, particularly in secondary school, can become quite challenging. Usually when the learner uses the same words a lot the spelling of the words can become more automatic – this is good as long as the word is spelled correctly.

This activity will help with the more complex words they come across in both primary and secondary school.

Good for...

Learners in secondary school but also upper stages of primary school.

Preparation/Materials

It is a good idea to look through your child's subject textbooks and try to extract some challenges and subject-specific words; for example, in science it might be the word 'anatomy'.

Teaching tip

It is a good idea to discuss the spelling strategies with your child. Try to get your child to come up with their own ideas.

Activity

Discuss this with your child and build up a bank of words for each subject. Some examples are shown below.

History	Geography	Chemistry	Biology
Agricultural	Climate	Chemical	Cell mutation
Conflict	Compass	Chloride	Chromosome
Dynasty	Continent	Compound	Cortex
Epoch	Environment	Experiment	Epidermis
Industrial	Equator	Hydrogen	Gyrus
Mariner	Forest	Organic	Mitosis
Monarch	Hemispheres	Potassium	Mutate
Parliament	Latitude	Soluble	Physiological
Pharaoh	Longitude	State	Protein
Revolution	Terrain	Weight	Stem
English	**Mathematics**	**Art**	**Physical education**
Adjective	Angular	Bronze	Coach
Description	Calculate	Distorted	Exercise
Dramatic	Equation	Easel	Line judge
Literature	Formulae	Photography	Muscles
Metaphor	Fraction	Sculpture	Physique
Poetic	Irregular	Sketch	Referee
Rhyme	Symbol	Texture	Spectator
Syntax	Symmetry	Vertical	Substitute

Music			
Bass Cymbals Musician Notes Orchestra Piano Saxophone Score sheet Treble Violin			

Select those words that your child finds challenging and ask them to compile a spelling vocabulary book with a separate page for different subjects. It could look something like this:

Subject	Word	Spelling tip	Meaning of word
Music	Bass	Remember the two s's	Deep sound from an instrument

Follow-up
This requires frequent revision.

Word toolbox
What words did your child learn today?

Additional resources
Look for visual spelling strategies: https://blog.allaboutlearningpress.com/effective-spelling-strategies

CHAPTER 5

Social and Emotional

It might be suggested that social and emotional factors are the most important aspects in relation to successful outcomes for the young person with dyslexia. Even the best reading and spelling programmes won't work as well if the child is not ready emotionally for learning.

It can also be suggested that group activities, if run appropriately, can be one of the best ways for the child to succeed. It is of course important that the young person feels at home and comfortable with the group and it is crucial if group activities are being carried out to ensure that is the case. Group activities can be a great leveller but conversely can be a great divider, and the youngster may feel inadequate in that particular group.

It is also important to consider and check that the learner is emotionally ready for learning. Children with dyslexia can have much to contend with and this can have an emotional impact. For that reason, we have included a number of activities to help stress-proof the child. We have activities on relaxation and physical and mental preparation for learning. We have tried to place ownership of this on the learner with activities such as a Body Check-In and Self-Care Checklist.

We have also added some very engaging activities for clearing the mind! Mindfulness features in some activities and this can also help the child deal with emotional issues. This type of activity can help the child talk about their concerns – this is important as children with dyslexia are often reluctant to talk about their worries. The Wall of Worries and Wall of Wisdom activity deals with this and can help to turn a negative into a positive. The activities Pump, Pedal, Glide and You Rock! can help to build positive and constructive strategies.

We would like your child to enjoy this chapter and of course it might be useful for all the family and friends!

ACTIVITIES

36. Body Check-In

Introduction
Often, children can feel themselves out of control in different situations. Children with attention or focus challenges also often struggle to maintain control of their bodies even when they try their hardest to sit still or stay in one spot. A great way to help your child gain some control and feel better about themselves is to walk them through the Body Check-In. This is a short script that you can either record and give to your child for them to use on their own or have them do it with you as you read the script. We have seen this work in real-life situations with the most challenging of students. Perhaps this is an activity that you can incorporate into your parenting toolbox to help your child gain some confidence and a sense of control over their own body.

Good for...
Children of any age.

Time frame
10–15 minutes.

Preparation/Materials
- Body Check-In script (below)
- A quiet place for your child to sit or lie down

Teaching tip
It's important to find the right time to introduce this activity to your child. As a parent, you can often see how your child's behaviour might be escalating and they are feeling out of control or you can sense that they need to slow down. This would be a good time to offer to do a check-in. In the middle of a meltdown or upsetting time would not be a good time, as your child will probably be beyond being able to calm themselves. Timing is important with this activity.

Activity

Once you have determined that it's a good time to introduce the activity, encourage your child to find a comfortable position anywhere in the room. Let them find their own position and their own place. Any position and any place is okay!

Begin reading the script slowly and deliberately with significant pauses between lines. Your child does not need to answer the questions, but encourage them to spend their time noticing their bodies as you continue reading the script.

Once you have finished reading, allow your child to 'come back to the room' and slowly get up from their position in their own time.

Follow-up

You can choose to play some ambient sounds or relaxing music during a Body Check-In to help create a calm environment. Some children find this helpful and some find it distracting. Experiment with your child and do what works for them.

Additional resources/ideas
Body Check-In script

Find a comfortable space on the floor or a bed or a chair – anywhere that feels comfortable for you. Take a deep breath. (PAUSE) Take another deep breath. (PAUSE)

Now, take a moment to feel your body and where it is in time and space. Feel your body connect with the surface that you are rested on. (PAUSE) Notice how your body feels as it touches and connects to the surface. Can you feel the surface on your back? Your legs? Your head? (PAUSE) Notice the qualities of the surface. Is the surface hard? Soft? (PAUSE) Notice if the surface has a temperature. Is it cool? Warm? (PAUSE)

Notice your eyes and if they are open or closed. (PAUSE) Experiment with them being either open or closed and then choose one that feels most comfortable to you, knowing that you can change at any time. (PAUSE)

Now, draw your attention to your feet. (PAUSE) Are they resting on anything? The floor, the bed, the chair, the couch, the grass perhaps? (PAUSE) Feel the surface beneath your feet and notice the quality of the surface. Is it hard or soft? Is it smooth or rough? Is it cool or warm? (PAUSE) Now, notice your feet and see if, without actually touching them, you can sense your toes. Are they tense or relaxed? (PAUSE) Can you get a sense of your toenails? (PAUSE) Can you tell you have toenails without touching them? (PAUSE)

Now, draw your attention to your (INSERT BODY PART). What is the surface it is resting on? (PAUSE) Notice how the surface feels. Is it soft or hard? (PAUSE) Is it cool or warm? (PAUSE) Is it rough or smooth? Does your (INSERT BODY PART) feel tense or relaxed? (PAUSE) Can you relax your (INSERT BODY PART) even more?

Continue with the above paragraph steps with as many body parts as you like (knees, thighs, hips/pelvis area, stomach, back, shoulders, elbows, hands, head).

Now take a moment to take a deep breath. Breathe in for four...1...2...3...4 and breathe out for four....1....2....3...4.

Repeat for three more breaths.

Now, start to slowly come back to the room. Slowly wiggle your toes and fingers. (PAUSE) Now slowly move your wrists and ankles. (PAUSE) Now slowly open your eyes if they are closed. (PAUSE) If they are open, slowly open and close your eyes. (PAUSE) Now roll to one side and take a breath. (PAUSE) Get up when you feel ready.

37. Self-Care Checklist

Introduction

This activity is one that will help your child learn more about themselves and care for themselves when they are feeling upset, overwhelmed or out of sorts. Quite often, when we are feeling uncomfortable emotions, we want to ignore them or keep ourselves busy so that we don't think about them. Helping your child create a list of self-soothing and self-care activities will help them get in tune with themselves and what brings them comfort, joy and peace. Once they have this list, they can refer to it whenever they are not feeling themselves.

Good for...
Children of any age.

Time frame
15–20 minutes to sit down with your child to brainstorm their activities with them.

Preparation/Materials

- A printout of the Self-Care Checklist (see the Appendix)
- Pen, pencil or colouring pencils
- A place to display the checklist in your child's room

Teaching tip

Working with your child on their Self-Care Checklist may also give you an opportunity to look at your own checklist. It can also be a great example and a lot of fun to do this *with* your child so that you can model the same self-care and self-awareness for them.

Activity

Sit down with your child and the checklist and brainstorm with them. Ask them what kinds of things they do that bring them safety, comfort, joy and pleasure. Ask them what kinds of things they do that help them to feel better when they're sad or upset. This may require some coaching from you as they might feel stumped to think of things. Activities can be as simple as...a hug from Mum or Dad, taking a bath, colouring, building LEGO®. It doesn't have to be a huge task; it just needs to be one that brings your child happiness, comfort, joy or pleasure.

Once you've come up with the list, the two of you can write them on your printed checklist. If your child can write, have them go ahead and do that. If they can't, they can draw pictures of the activity or you can print some pictures off the internet to help with visuals.

38. Calendar Themes

Introduction

Every person needs a little motivation and at times this can be a challenge. What better way to inspire a child than by getting them to create their own personalized calendar which highlights special moments for them and helps them home in on positive messages and themes that are important for them? They can celebrate themselves or any their friends and family as well as choose inspiring messages to keep them going when times get rough.

Good for...

Children of all ages. It also helps with boosting self-confidence, self-esteem and their sense of resiliency. It allows children to choose important messages and themes that resonate and inspire them.

Time frame

Typically, this would be a project for a weekend or perhaps may even be spread out over the course of a week. It's a perfect craft project for the winter or half-term holidays when your child has time to be crafty!

Preparation/Materials

Twelve photos chosen by your child. Each photo should be meaningful to them in some way. Photos can include family, friends, pets, pictures – whatever they find inspiring and helpful. Each month should include a theme, such as friendship, sharing, gratitude. These are just suggestions but these themes should be important to your child. Within the calendar days of the week, you can create your own special holidays and days that specifically celebrate or encourage your theme.

Teaching tip

While your child is creating their calendar, make one for yourself to model and highlight the purpose of the activity. Choose photos and themes important to you and create your own holidays and special days as well. This project can easily be a family project completed as a unit, or a special activity that results in each family member creating their own calendar and inspirational moments as well!

Activity

Choose a theme and a photo that celebrates each month. Create your own special holidays or days within the calendar month and ask your child to focus on this theme for that particular month. Take care to hang up the calendar in a place where they can see it – bedrooms are ideal, but the kitchen and family room work as well. If your child is especially artistic, allow them to decorate their own calendar or even design images in lieu of photos. The purpose of this activity is to get them thinking of concepts and ideas that are important to them and that they might want to get more experience of practising.

Follow-up

Build your own themed calendar.

39. You Rock!

Introduction

We all need inspiration and help motivating ourselves from time to time, and this particular activity helps to achieve this in a fun and artistic way. You can do it individually or you can do it as a family and as a way to support and mentor your children when the going gets tough. By creating visual reminders, you can provide encouragement when things seem impossible, or recognize a job well done without the fuss and fanfare that can sometimes take over our actions. During the COVID-19 pandemic, there was a trend of people decorating beautiful stones with inspirational messages for times of uncertainty. It's these little messages of hope and wisdom that can sometimes inspire us to do better or hang in there when our own sense of motivation is lagging.

Good for...
Creating resilience, self-esteem, metacognition, self-awareness, perspective taking.

Time frame
Whenever needed – this activity is child–parent focused and can be used whenever needed.

Preparation/Materials

- Ten pebbles of a medium size
- Metallic markers to decorate the pebbles
- A basket for storing pebbles

Activity
With your child, create a set of stones with personal and motivating messages on them aimed at inspiring or recognizing goodness in ourselves or in other family members. Make them beautiful and readable. The messages on these pebbles can really home in on skills that you want to encourage your child to develop so that these messages will eventually turn into positive habits. Some ideas for messages include:

Focus

Be kind

Wow!

Take your time

Be helpful

Nice job!

Celebrate

Inspire

Be joyful

Amazing

Be you

You rock!

Manners

Just breathe

Kindness

Energize

Display these stones in the basket, somewhere where they are accessible so that family members can choose pebbles they would like to use themselves or encourage others to adopt. For example, you might want to put a pebble in your child's lunch box, on their bed, next to their spot at the table. Also, children should be encouraged to choose pebbles with messages that they might want to work on such as 'Quiet', 'Focus' or 'Just breathe'. Like all good skills and habits, it's important for parents to model the use of them and be seen using them for themselves but also to use them in appropriate moments for other family members. Encourage your child to send a positive message to siblings and friends so that they can see how important it is to have a positive attitude but also that it is important to support and encourage everyone in their own struggles and challenges.

Follow-up
Use these pebbles for as long as you need to until you notice a change in habits and attitudes.

40. Just Breathe

Introduction
Our breath is something that we carry with us on a daily basis, and we often take for granted the many uses that it serves. The recent fascination with mindfulness has helped us as a society to see the benefits in creating body awareness for our children and how it can help them to relax, be mindful and regulate themselves. This simple technique is useful for everyone, but especially important for children who are just learning how to emotionally regulate themselves and take responsibility for their actions.

Good for...
Social/emotional regulation, impulse control, meditation, body awareness.

Time frame

10 minutes before bedtime, or in any situation where a child feels a pause is needed before proceeding with a thought or action.

Preparation/Materials

Just your breath!

Teaching tip

Start small and be consistent. Adopt it as part of something bigger, such as bedtime routine, so that kids can make connections between their breath and things that they might struggle with.

Activity

Because this activity is so simple, it's worthwhile taking the time to develop it and teach children the intention behind doing it. By taking the time to be aware of your breath, a child can learn about their own emotional state as well as how certain breathing techniques are helpful when they are feeling overwhelmed, stressed, anxious or need a 'reset' moment. A good way to introduce this activity is just before bed. Sit with your child, and simply practise five minutes of intentional awareness aimed at monitoring your breath. You can sit cross-legged on the floor in a quiet space and just practise being aware of your breath. This includes paying attention to how your breathing feels in your nose, how your body feels breathing and the rhythm that it creates. Pay attention to how it feels to sit quietly without disruptions – does it feel comfortable, uncomfortable? Take the time to develop this practice and encourage a moment of solitude for your child.

Once you have mastered this technique, you can practise using your breath in a different way. Another favourite use of the breath is when a child is feeling emotionally overwhelmed. This may be triggered by a person or a situation. Encourage your child to use their breath as a way to emotionally 'reset' before proceeding with an action. For example, this might be, 'Take five deep breathes before you say something,' or 'Take eight deep breathes before you do your maths test.' You can also encourage your child to use their breath as a way to engage with their life and take a moment so that they can have more control of their emotions and actions.

Follow-up

Square breathing, pizza breathing. For example, see: www.youtube.com/watch?v=WMmrJp5q5OQ

Word toolbox

What words did your child learn today? Start with self-regulation, impulse control.

Additional resources

www.parents.com/fun/activities/5-mindfulness-activities-you-can-do-as-a-family

https://blissfulkids.com/how-to-practice-mindfulness-with-children-the-essential-guide

41. Wall of Worries and Wall of Wisdom

Introduction

Quite often, children with dyslexia and other learning differences can experience feelings of anxiety and worry. Creating a Wall of Worries and a Wall of Wisdom can help children to get in tune with their thoughts and feelings, write them down so that they are out of their heads, and then think about a positive or wise thought to replace the worry thought.

Good for...

Children of any age.

Time frame

Five minutes to prepare and print off the Wall of Worries and Wall of Wisdom worksheets (see the Appendix) (longer if you'd like to create your own). 30 minutes or more for the activity itself.

Preparation/Materials

- Pen or pencil
- A printout of the worksheet
- Blank paper if your child wants to create their own page
- Coloured pencils or pens or felt pens to draw pictures
- Sticky notes

Teaching tip

An example worry might be: 'I am worried that I won't do well in my test tomorrow.' An example wise or positive thought might be: 'I can try my very best and that is always good enough.'

Activity

Ask your child to take a few deep breaths and think about a thought or a worry that has been weighing heavily on their mind. Your child can then write that thought on a sticky note and stick it to the Wall of Worries. They can post as many worries as they have. Once your child has posted all of their worries on the wall, they then can think about a wise or positive thought to replace that worry, write it down and then stick it to the Wall of Wisdom.

Follow-up

If you find that your child encounters worries throughout the day, encourage them to write them down on a sticky note and save them for 'Worry Time' when you can sit down with them and go over these worries and put them up on the Worry Wall. Once you have done that, you can address the worry by coming up with a wise or positive thought to counter the worry.

Word toolbox

Sometimes it is difficult for children to come up with the words for their worries or anxieties. Help them to find the words by asking them to describe their thoughts, sensations in their bodies, possible colours, temperatures and shapes of what they are feeling. This can help them put words and language to their sometimes overwhelming and confusing worries or thoughts.

Additional resources/ideas

Worries and anxiety can present differently in all children. Another fun activity is making your own worry dolls. These can easily be created and your child can use them to tell their worries to See: https://my-little-poppies.com/make-your-own-worry-dolls

42. Mindfulness Jar

Introduction

These days children can easily become overwhelmed by all of the stimulus around them. Many children can be reactive and have little self-control over their feelings. Mindfulness is a technique that is garnering momentum and is teaching young kids to become more empowered by their thoughts and feelings and helping them to cope with daily stressors. Creating a Mindfulness Jar is a way to start encouraging kids to be mindful of their thoughts and emotions while allowing them to have some control over their expression of these emotions.

Good for...

Any child who struggles with self-regulation, difficult emotions or impulse control.

Time frame

10–15 minutes daily, or whenever your child feels the need to be calm or take some time to sit out and learn to breathe and gain more control over their emotions.

Preparation/Materials

- A glass jar, lid included
- Glitter glue – colour of choice
- Food colouring
- Additional glitter if desired
- Warm water

To make your Mindfulness Jar, add your preferred colour of glitter glue to the jar, then add additional glitter if desired, top up with warm water, add a few drops of food colouring and then close the jar with the lid. Seal tightly and allow the warm water to dissolve the glitter glue, leaving only sparkles. After an hour or overnight, you will have a Mindfulness Jar.

Teaching tip

Model this technique for your child and use it consistently and daily in order for your child to become accustomed to using it.

Activity

You can use this jar for multiple purposes. Some children have difficulty falling asleep at night. Have them shake the jar and practise some breathing exercises as they watch the glitter fall to the bottom of the jar. Have them repeat this several times until their breathing is regular and they feel relaxed. For kids who have difficulty settling into a task or their homework, have them use the Mindfulness Jar in the same way. Have them shake the jar and breathe as the glitter falls to the bottom. You may want them to repeat this activity five times before they start on their homework.

The simple act of breathing helps to create a sense of calm and allows them to engage in a task. This activity is also helpful for emotional outbursts from children. They can simply have time out, sit and breathe and then you can discuss what went wrong and try to get to the bottom of the problem. This activity is intended to create space by breathing and allow your child to calm down and think about an issue or problem they may be having.

Follow-up
Other mindful activities which might be useful.

Additional resources
www.firefliesandmudpies.com/glitter-timers
www.youtube.com/watch?v=nP9YP5Yg1qI

43. Pump, Pedal, Glide

Introduction
The importance of teaching our children the art of resilience and how to acquire grit is a much-discussed issue in our current times. As a society, we are increasingly becoming aware of the value of social intelligence and all of the factors that go into making a successful individual. Resilience and grit are two key terms that have long been associated with dyslexia, and the explicit teaching of these skills has become the focus of many forms of intervention. The following activity aims to teach you how to build both resilience and grit and how to keep motivation going for your child even in the most challenging of times.

Good for...
Building motivation and self-awareness. Builds metacognition and executive functioning, establishes forms of resilience and teaches how to build grit. To be used with mostly with older students aged 10–18 years. However, it can be adapted for younger students.

Time frame
10–15 minutes each night.

Preparation/Materials

A printout of the worksheet for recording moments and situations (see the Appendix).

Teaching tip

Be consistent in using this activity. It's important that children can see their own strengths and weaknesses and act on them.

Activity

The basis of this activity is to create an awareness within your child of the struggles they may encounter in their daily lives. For example, children need to be aware of both their individual strengths and weaknesses and how to work with them on a daily basis. They need to learn how to reflect honestly on these issues and come up with their own forms of compensatory mechanisms that will help them deal with their 'weaknesses' while celebrating and recognizing their strengths.

The idea behind the phrase 'pump, pedal, glide' is to raise an awareness of situations when they might have to 'pump' (really try hard and come up with strategies to get through a situation), 'pedal' (work at an even pace – not too hard, not too easy) and when they get to 'glide' (take advantage of their strengths to enjoy the moment and celebrate their success when something is easy for them or they have produced an outstanding piece of work that was effortless). Recording and becoming more aware of when they need to work harder or when they can relax and enjoy their moment is a useful skill for dyslexic children to learn. It allows them to acquire and build strategies that work for them and be aware of how their strengths serve them in their daily interactions.

As a parent using this activity, it's important that you model its use and once you use it with your child, be sure to have a discussion about why it's important. For example, for a child who struggles with homework and can identify it, it might help them build strategies that will compensate for this, such as start earlier in the day, do a little bit each day, ask for help, work with a homework buddy. By recognizing where they need to 'pump', they have the opportunity to change or help themselves.

Follow-up

View some TED talks on motivation and grit.

Word toolbox

What words did your child learn today? Start with motivation, resilience, grit.

Additional resources

www.ted.com/talks/angela_lee_duckworth_grit_the_power_of_passion_and_perseverance

44. Talking Stick for Conflict Resolution

Introduction

Inevitably, families have conflicts. How a family navigates conflict and uncomfortable situations can make a huge difference in how our children handle conflict outside the home. A great way to introduce and encourage healthy conflict and conflict resolution is to introduce a Talking Stick. This encourages active listening – a skill that helps build trust and understanding during times of conflict.

Good for...

Children and adults of any age.

Time frame

30 minutes or more for stick creation.

Preparation/Materials

- A stick or plastic wand or any stick-like item that you can decorate
- Construction paper
- Feathers, beads, stickers, glue and so on
- A dedicated Talking Toy Animal or Talking Spoon if you are not creating your own stick

Activity

Listening is an often underrated skill when it comes to conflict. You might think that listening is a fairly straightforward act of simply being quiet and letting the other person speak. Active listening is something quite different. Active listening is when your attention is dedicated solely to the other person and what they are saying and you are looking to understand that person. It takes practice to hone the skill of active listening. A family Talking Stick can help you and your child develop this skill.

During a calm time within the family, bring the members together and introduce the concept of the Talking Stick. The idea is to have a dedicated item that the family can use in times of conflict. When one of the family members is holding the stick, that is *their* time to speak. No one else is allowed to speak. The other members of the family must actively listen to the person speaking and dedicate their whole selves to listening and trying to understand what the person is saying. When the person is finished, the stick gets passed to the next member and the same thing happens for that person until all members have been heard.

Active listening is about listening to understand, and once a person feels understood and heard, then it becomes easier to develop ways to resolve the conflict peacefully.

Follow-up

If creating your own Talking Stick feels too onerous, feel free to find a favourite toy animal or a wooden spoon or other household item to use as your Talking Stick. It doesn't have to be fancy. The idea is to have some physical item for a family member to hold while they are speaking.

Additional resources/ideas

The principle of the Talking Stick comes from many Indigenous cultures. To find out more about the protocol and how it is used in First Nations cultures, take a look at: www.ictinc.ca/blog/first-nation-talking-stick-protocol

45. Family Values Board

Introduction

What are values? Know it or not, everyone operates on their own set of values. To help our children feel a sense of belonging and community, finding out your values and creating a Family Values Board or manifesto is a great way to encourage them to learn to become a part of a whole and find out what is important to them and to their family.

Good for...

Children and adults of any age.

Time frame

An hour or more for the family brainstorm. Another hour or more to create your own Family Values Board or manifesto.

Preparation/Materials

- Pen, pencils, colouring pencils, felt markers
- Paper
- Large cardstock or poster paper
- Computer and printer (if creating your board digitally)

Teaching tip

Many sources advise looking at a list of values and picking your favourite ones from that list. While this can be helpful, discovering your values can be more meaningful when you think about things that you don't like or things that bother you. For example, if someone really doesn't like lying, then honesty would be a value for them, or if someone doesn't like to be lazy, they might value activity or adventure. Explore both ways of discovering your family values and see what works for you.

Activity

Sit down with your family and introduce the concept of creating your Family Values Board. Explain that this will help everyone be more aware of what is important in your lives and feel as if they are part of a community with common goals and values.

Brainstorm and ask all or some of the following questions:

- What's important to us as a family?
- When do we feel the most satisfied or alive?
- How do we make difficult decisions?
- What are some things that we don't like or things that bother us? (The opposite will usually spark a value for you)
- What achievement are we most proud of?
- What do we daydream about?

Some sample values could be:

- Honesty
- Dependability
- Flexibility
- Loyalty
- Commitment
- Openness
- Authenticity
- Compassion
- Contribution

- Creativity
- Humour
- Peace
- Fun

Find the values that you all agree on and feel good about. Once you have done this, you're ready to create your board or manifesto. You can create this in many different ways. Do an internet search for 'family values' and you will find some good examples. You can start the board out with any one of the following statements:

- 'In our home, we believe…'
- 'In this house, we…'
- 'We believe…'

If you are technologically savvy, you can use different software programs to create your own digital manifesto and print it out. If you're going low-tech, create your handwritten and hand-drawn poster. This alone can be a fun family activity where members can add drawings and put their own unique 'stamp' on the board.

Display the poster or board somewhere in a main part of your household for every member to see.

Follow-up

It's important to remember that values are not a static thing. Values can change. Revisit your family values every year or so. A great tradition could be to have a family values meeting on New Year's Day to kick off the new year with a renewed sense of purpose and passion.

Additional resources/ideas

Feel free to use the example included in the Appendix or use it as a guide to create your own unique Family Values Board. Most importantly, have fun!

CHAPTER 6

Executive Functioning

This term – executive functioning – may be new to some parents. It is, however, an important component of learning, and challenges with executive functioning can be evident in children with dyslexia. Executive functioning is the engine of the brain – it can control and regulate activities and is a powerful part of learning. It can deal with organizing, prioritizing work, focusing, sustained attention, and adjusting processing speed depending on the task. It also deals with managing frustration and regulating emotions as well as self-regulation and self-monitoring. Executive functioning also includes both working memory and long-term memory. Many of these areas can be affected for children and young people with dyslexia.

You can see that this incorporates a wide range of areas and therefore the activities in this chapter are quite wide-ranging but they can be very effective for children with dyslexia. We have a number of activities on memory strategies and organization. We also look at planning and have included activities that can help with homework. The rationale underpinning many of these activities is to promote independence in the young person. To take control of their own learning is one of the key pathways to success.

ACTIVITIES

46. Organizing Passport

Introduction

For some children, organizing their daily life with routines and habits can be a real challenge. At times, children may forget to do the most basic elements of their day – brush their teeth, pack their bag, make their bed. In order for children to learn to have more control over their day and be more independent, they need to learn to create habits and routines. An Organizing Passport helps make this process less painful and rewards children for the effort and time they spend creating new habits. This style of teaching habits is both positive and motivating and will help your child learn the much-needed skills of being an organized person.

Good for...

Any child who forgets things or seems overwhelmed by their daily routine.

Time frame

Initially, this should take 30–60 minutes – this will include explanations on how it works and perhaps modelling the procedure. After regular use it should take 10–15 minutes a day. Consistency is key for this activity.

Preparation/Materials

Depending on your child an organizational chart of 'routines' they need to work on (see the Appendix), and stickers.

Teaching tip

Keep it simple and keep the same routine. Check the chart before bed or at a key time in the day. Be sure to follow up and then give them the job of checking in with you to share their success and jobs for the day. While it may seem that it is more work at the start, this activity pays dividends once it is established.

Activity

With your child, draw up a chart of their routines and tasks to be accomplished each day. Tell your child they are now going to be in charge of their day and that at the end of the day, you will be checking in to see if they have completed what needed to be done. Explain to them that for every job they have accomplished, you will put a star on their passport. Once they have filled up their passport, they will 'earn' a reward. The reward is to be established by you and is unknown to your child. This keeps interest high, but the reward is something that is personal and meaningful. Not every child will have the same style or elements to their day. For younger children, be sure to use an aid that is helpful and age appropriate. Examples of routine schedules aimed at different age groups are covered in the Create and Set Up Routines activity.

Follow-up

After the child has filled in their first passport, have a candid discussion about how it feels to be more 'in charge' of their day. Take the time to discuss the pros and cons and be sure to give specific feedback to your child. This might be, 'I notice that you are happier in the mornings because you aren't so rushed' or 'I love the fact that you can be organized as it allows me to be more organized too.' The key to this activity is positive reinforcement until it becomes a habit.

47. Whiteboard System Central for Families

Introduction

Students who struggle with executive functioning skills do best when things are laid out for them and routines are clear and known. Having a whiteboard in a central area of the home that details routines, chores and schedules can be an excellent way to help your child keep on track with their schedules and your expectations for them. It's also a great way to encourage them through messages, notes and the like.

Good for...

Families with children of any age.

Time frame

About an hour to set the whiteboard up. About 10 minutes each day to update the schedule.

Preparation/Materials

- A medium to large whiteboard or whiteboard calendar with space to write additional notes
- Whiteboard dry-erase markers (different colours)
- Sticky notes (optional)
- Whiteboard eraser
- Jotted notes of what you want to include on the whiteboard (some suggestions are: calendar, each member's daily schedule, each member's daily chores, motivating or inspiring quotes, messages for members of the family, before and after school routines, meal plans)

Activity

Once you've got your materials, find a place in your home where every family member congregates. This is often the kitchen or dining area. The goal here is to find a place where all members can and will see the whiteboard on a regular basis.

Map out the calendar and put important dates and appointments on there for each day. Detail each person's daily schedule and routines. It's a good idea to detail your child's routine expectations for before and after school and have them check off the tasks as they finish them.

Include personal messages for family members and inspirational or motivational quotes to help them feel connected to each other and inspired to keep checking back.

Follow-up

While this may seem like a basic concept, it can be extremely helpful for children who struggle with executive functioning skills and those who need structure to their days. It's a wonderful way to help children get in the habit of checking in with themselves and their tasks for the day and it will help to give them a sense of accomplishment.

Homework Work Station

Introduction

This is the activity for you if you have young children at home who enjoy arts and crafts and would like to learn to be more in charge of their space and learning. This activity involves children at each stage of the organizational set-up. First, they get to create a highly personalized organizational tool, and second, it helps them to order and arrange their preferred style of working and ensures they have everything they need to complete the job successfully.

Good for...

Younger children who struggle to make sure they have all the tools they will need to do their nightly homework. This activity may be adapted for older students as well, but instead of 'making' the tool, they can shop for their preferred objects and create the ultimate desk set-up.

Time frame

It will take up to two hours to create this work station box. It depends on how long your child spends decorating and setting up their work space afterwards.

Preparation/Materials

- An empty tissue box or shoe box
- Toilet rolls
- Small empty boxes
- Scissors
- Decorating paper, markers, glue, tape

Teaching tip

This is a very motivating activity that can easily be completed within a couple of hours on a rainy afternoon. Kids love to make and create things and they are keen to use it because they have created it!

Activity

After you have gathered the necessary materials, tell your child you are going to create a Homework Work Station to ensure that they have everything they need. Have your child select the paper with which they can wrap or decorate the empty box. It can be plain paper, left-over wrapping paper, anything that creates interest. If you are using an old tissue box, you will need to cut the top off so that you have room for the toilet rolls. Next, you will need to measure and figure out how many empty toilet rolls you will need: one for pencils, one for markers, one for rulers and so on. Help your child colour or decorate them. Once decorated, tie a string around them to secure them and place them in the box. Next, you need to decide how many smaller boxes will fit and what you will put in them. Perhaps one for pens and one for the small items such as erasers.

Once you have decorated your box and decided on the smaller boxes, you need to fill it with all the items your child uses in order to successfully have all of their tools to hand to do their homework. You might want to complete a list and fill the box with all of these items.

Ideally, it would be great to put this on your child's desk and have it stay there for working purposes, but the beauty of this homework box is that it can travel to wherever your child is working. For example, if they have an online tutoring session, they can bring the box with them to ensure that they have everything they need for the class. It is a versatile tool that helps ensure that they are not running about the house looking for a pencil before their online session or that they have everything they need before settling down to do their nightly homework.

Additional resources

www.youtube.com/watch?v=aWJ6xvWW1H0
https://whatmomslove.com/kids/how-to-create-ultimate-homework-station

49. Craft Stick Chores

Introduction
Have you ever argued with your child about them being more responsible around the house or wish that they would be more independent in organizing themselves day to day? This is an activity that you can try in order for them to complete their chores successfully with as little fuss as possible. It is quick, efficient and takes away the tendency to procrastinate when it is time to do a chore. The activity can be used with the entire family and maintains a sense of fairness and freshness when it is time to contribute to household chores.

Good for...
Organizing, independence, self-esteem, resilience, team building, cooperation.

Time frame
20 minutes a day.

Preparation/Materials

- Craft sticks
- A small container with sand
- A small empty jar for putting sticks in once chore is complete
- A chart for keeping track of chores

Teaching tip

If your child struggles with getting ready in the morning or organizing themselves for school, this activity can be adapted for use by a single person. You can write individual steps and colour code them on sticks in order to help your child learn to be independent and create routines. For example, you can have an assortment of coloured sticks. All of the orange sticks must be completed before your child leaves for school in the morning – getting dressed, brushing teeth, washing face, packing bag, packing lunch and so on. Blue sticks can be after-school chores that must be completed before they have 'free time' – unpack bag, get changed into after-school clothes, do homework, have snack.

Activity

On the craft sticks, simply write the chores that you wish to achieve either each day or each week and then put them chore side down in the container with the sand so that no one can see what is written on the stick. You can colour code the sticks and have a certain colour for each family member, or you can just have regular sticks with chores. This activity works best when you set parameters or a schedule. For example, if your family is rushed in the morning, don't bother with it in the morning. Save it for after school when there is naturally more time and your family members don't feel pressurized. The idea is to create a habit so it works best at the same time either every day or set to a certain schedule.

Each family member pulls a stick from the container and then completes the task written on it. For example, empty the dishwasher, tidy the kitchen worktops, put shoes in the front cupboard, set the table for dinner, walk the dog. You can customize it to the chores that typically need to be done around the house. Make sure there is a good selection of chores to be done and that they are doable for your family members. You are aiming at teaching responsibility and teamwork, so success is key here. Also, as a nice surprise, you can include sticks such as: take the day off, switch sticks with Mum, pay yourself an extra three happy faces for doing your chores.

Follow-up

If you wish, you can start a family tracker whereby each time a family member does a chore, they put a tick mark or a happy face on the chart. Once you reach a certain amount, you can reward them with a family treat such as a trip for an ice-cream, a family movie with popcorn or pizza, a game night – something that is interesting for everyone and something that is done as a family unit.

50. Frame It!

Introduction

Decisions can be hard to make and it is often tricky to see the impact of the decisions we make on a daily basis. For some children, decision making is not a thoughtful process but rather a hasty or snap decision they make on the spur of an emotion or feeling, with little attention paid to the outcome. Making thoughtful decisions is a skill, and one that needs to be practised numerous times in a multitude of ways so that children can become balanced decision makers. Adults will recognize this activity as weighing up the pros and cons of a decision. For the purpose of this activity, we are merely framing thoughts and choosing the best one with the most desirable outcome.

Good for...

Children aged 9–17 years. Executive planning, weighing outcomes, planning for the future, engaging decision making, delaying gratification, recognizing the impact of decisions.

Time frame

Ideally, this activity should take between eight and ten minutes, but may take longer at the start to model the decision-making process.

Preparation/Materials

- A printout of the Frame It! worksheet (see the Appendix)
- Pencil or pen

Teaching tip

Model a few scenarios with some hypothetical problems that are similar to decisions your own child is faced with. After you've done a few, your child will understand the importance of making wise decisions and see the process involved in making good decisions. It's not just the outcome you want to highlight, but more importantly the process itself.

Activity

This is an exercise in externalizing your thoughts and coming to the best possible outcome. By looking at both sides of the decision, children can see all the choices they have, but focus on choosing the most desirable outcome after weighing up all of their options. At the top of the page, write down the decision or problem your child may be encountering. As your child begins to verbalize their thought process, ask them which frame that thought should be put in. Ask why it goes there and discuss why it belongs there. Once you have several options for each frame, ask your child which one they would like to choose and why. Discuss the ramifications of the choice – the good things that come out of it or the consequences of making a poor choice. This externalizing of thinking should help children see the ultimate actions that occur as a result of making any decision.

Additional resources

www.kiddiematters.com/problem-solving-activity-free-printable

https://choices.scholastic.com/content/dam/classroom-magazines/choices/issues/2016-17/050117/
how-can-i-make-a---tough-decision--/CHO-050117-DECISION-DecisionMakingGrid.pdf

51. Tag It! Backpack Tags

Introduction

How many times has your child come home from school saying that they forgot their homework or their lunch box or their PE clothes? It can be a very common refrain with children, especially those who struggle with executive functioning and organizational skills. Creating a customized tag for your child's backpack can be an excellent way to help take a few moments at the end of their school day to check in and collect all of their necessary homework items and other things before they leave school and come home.

Good for...
School-aged children.

Time frame

Up to 30 minutes to create and attach tag. About three to four minutes for your child to check their tag every day at the end of their school day.

Preparation/Materials

- A printout of the included tag or your own tag, printed on heavy-duty cardstock (see the Appendix)

- If you have a laminator, one lamination sheet and your laminator
- A hole punch to make a hole at the top of the tag
- A small keyring

Activity

Make a list of the things that you want to help your child remember to bring home or to check on before they leave school. You can also take this opportunity to engage with your child and get their feedback on what they think they need to have on the tag. Feel free to use the BagTag supplied (in the Appendix) if you feel that will work for your family, or go ahead and make your own. Print off your BagTag on heavy cardstock. Laminate the card with your own laminator. If you do not have a laminator, we strongly suggest having the tag laminated at your local print shop so that the tag can remain durable throughout the year. Once laminated, make a hole at the top of the tag to put a small keyring through it. If lamination isn't an option, use a simple luggage tag and write out a tag and slide it into the luggage tag. Attach the tag to a part of your child's backpack where it is easy to see.

Follow-up

Take some time with your child to go through the BagTag and explain the purpose of the tag to them. Have them involved in the process of making the tag and decorating it however they want to by adding stickers or drawings of their own. Having some ownership of the tag might help them feel more engaged with it and its purpose.

52. Rewind! Looking Back at the Day

Introduction

This is a quick and easy activity that you can do with your child in order to be reflective and recognize patterns. It really just requires some time at the end of the day to think about your day – to rewind it – and come up with something positive about it or something that you might do differently if presented with the opportunity to do so.

Good for...

Social/emotional regulation, metacognition and behaviour. It also creates resilience and perspective taking.

Time frame

20 minutes at the end of the day.

Preparation/Materials

- Pen or pencil
- Sticky notes as reminders

Teaching tip

Model this activity every night with your child for a month and then simply provide a visual reminder for them to think about on their own. This can be as simple as a drawing with the word 'rewind' on it in order to create the habit.

Activity

This activity is best done at the end of the day with your child in order to model and teach the skill of self-reflection.

With most children, they will benefit from you modelling this skill first. Here are some suggested prompts:

- Today I wish I had _____ because
- When I look back at today, I feel_____ because
- I had a great day because_____
- I had a tough day because_____
- If I could change one thing about today, I would _____

Follow-up

Try to integrate this skill every night as part of a night-time routine until it becomes a habit or it seems more natural. Keep it simple and always allow your child to express their thoughts without judgement or as something that needs to be 'fixed'. Allow your child to think through their behaviour chains or triggers of the day and use helpful prompts to encourage them to develop their own thinking or way of changing a situation.

Word toolbox

What words did your child learn today? Start with metacognition, behaviour chain, thoughts.

53. Family Time Capsule

Introduction

This is a great family activity that encourages planning, creating and executing a task. It is a wonderful way for the family to get involved in planning and creating and can be done on a regular basis throughout your child's life. An activity like this can help children make a plan, find things that they want to include, research what has been happening in their world, and think about who they are and what their likes and dislikes are currently.

Good for...

Families with children of any age.

Time frame

Up to two hours to write up your part of the capsule. About one to two hours to collect the items for the capsule. About 15 minutes to share everything with each other, fill the capsule and bury it.

Preparation/Materials

- A large jar or plastic container
- Photos that you would like to include
- Some of your children's artwork
- Movie tickets or event tickets such as concerts
- Small toys such as LEGO® figures
- Copies of newspaper articles or headlines
- Paints and paper to create your handprints
- Computer to research current prices and time-sensitive things

Teaching tip

This is a great opportunity to sit down with your child and reflect on the last few years. What things were happening in the world that they thought were big or impactful? What are some events they attended that were noteworthy? What things are they most proud of?

Activity

In order to prepare for this activity, have your child answer some of the following questions:

1. What is my favourite toy?
2. What is my favourite colour?
3. What is my favourite food?
4. What is my favourite book or books?
5. What is my favourite music or song?
6. What is my favourite game?
7. What is my favourite TV programme or movie?
8. What do I want to be when I grow up?
9. Who are my friends?
10. What is the one thing that I like the most about myself?
11. What is my favourite thing to do?
12. What do I want to be when I grow up?

Adults can consider the following questions:

1. What is my favourite colour?
2. What is my favourite food?
3. What is my favourite book or books?
4. What is my favourite music or song?
5. Where would I like to travel?
6. What is my favourite TV programme or movie?
7. What is the one thing that I like the most about myself?
8. What is my favourite thing to do?
9. What are my goals for the next year? The next five years?

Have each family member write down their favourite memories from the last year or five years. Have each family member write a letter to their future selves. Make handprints of your hands. Jot down current prices for homes, petrol/diesel, loaves of bread, milk cartons and eggs, popular music, movies, TV shows, current events.

Follow-up

This is an activity that you can revisit every couple of years or even up to every five to ten years. Dig up the capsule, open it and read it together as a family. Create new things to add to the capsule and revisit your questions every time you open it.

Additional resources/ideas

To access a free download of printable sheets for your time capsule, visit: https://playfulnotes.com/family-time-capsule

54. Geocaching: The World's Largest Treasure Hunt

Introduction

Treasure hunts have been around for years but did you know that there is a worldwide treasure hunt that you and your child can enjoy? Geocaching is the world's largest treasure hunt that people have been playing for quite a while now. Treasure hunting involves many executive functioning skills such as planning, inferring clues, map reading and navigation. This fun activity can be a great way to help your child develop their executive functioning skills and have fun at the same time!

Good for...

Families with children of any age.

Time frame

The time possibilities are endless!

Preparation/Materials

- A smartphone
- The Geocaching app
- GPS
- Pen and paper
- Knick-knack or item to trade (optional)

Activity

Geocaching is a collective treasure hunt activity. There are thousands of Geocaching treasures hidden all over the world. Download the free app onto your smartphone and you're ready to go! This is a great family activity to help your children engage in working out clues, navigation and problem solving.

Follow-up

Treasure hunts can also be created in your own home! Have your child create their own treasure hunt and let you find the treasure.

Additional resources/ideas

www.geocaching.com/play

A great resource for creating your own 'at-home' treasure hunt: https://playtivities.com/at-home-treasure-hunt

55. Time to Focus

Introduction

We are sure that you will be aware that your child can have difficulty focusing when they are tackling difficult tasks like reading or writing. It is important this is considered and some strategies are put in place to minimize the impact of it.

One of the important points that will be covered in this activity is to get the environment and the task right to help with focusing.

Good for...

Children of any age.

Time frame

This should not take long but it is worthwhile spending some time on it as it can be helpful for all tasks and activities.

Preparation/Materials

The activity is all about preparation; no additional materials are needed.

Teaching tip

You may find the ten points below may have to be adapted for different learners. Try to tailor them to your child.

Activity

Ten simple but important tips:

1. Clear your child's desk – make sure there are no obvious distractions, especially pencils, pencil sharpeners, rulers and so on.

2. Consider some music – this should be very much background music and not interfere with focusing or learning.

3. Think about the lighting – is it too bright or too dark? It's a good idea to use a table lamp and switch off the main light.

4. Do one task at a time – if it is a long task, break it into sections. Focus only on the task at hand and not what has still to be done.

5. Try to make sure the task is quite short and achievable. It is very important that your child should be able to complete the task.

6. Allow frequent breaks – short tasks and frequent breaks are best.

7. Show achievement – it is a good idea if your child has some sort of progress sheet and can tick off tasks that have been completed. They need to know that they are improving and they need to see this – a chart is a good way of doing this.

8. Provide feedback immediately they complete the task – try to provide elaborate and specific feedback, by explaining why something is good.

9. Review what your child has done and highlight this, indicating how they can use this new learning.

10. Celebrate success – remember that positive self-esteem is important for all aspects of learning and this includes focusing.

Follow-up

Knowing your child's learning style can also help with focusing. Have a look at some websites on learning styles, such as: www.time4learning.com/learning-styles

Word toolbox

What words did your child learn today?

Learning chart

Prompt your child to record their learning.

Today I learned _____

Additional resources

Tips for concentration: www.oxfordlearning.com/how-to-help-child-focus-in-school

56. Improve Your Memory: Chunk It!

Introduction

Memory is important for learning, although it should *not* replace understanding. Children and young people with dyslexia may have some challenges with memory and may forget important information. They often have more challenges with short-term memory than long-term memory, but one can lead to difficulties in the other. It is important that new information is processed and one of the most effective ways of doing that is for the learner to take control of the learning process themselves. This has implications for how they memorize information. For that reason, memory strategies are important.

Good for...

All ages, perhaps more for teens.

Time frame

Around one hour to practise this, but daily practice is important too.

Preparation/Materials

Ask your child to think of some items they want to remember – perhaps dates from a history lesson, or names of their favourite football team or the grocery list!

Teaching tip

It is a good idea to get them to start with a random list of items and then chunk them once the list is completed. This formula can be useful:

1. List.
2. Pattern – look for similarities.
3. Chunk.

Activity

Preparing to go on holiday provides an opportunity to encourage your child to take some responsibility for organization and memory. Helping them to pack can be a memory and organization activity.

You can do this by introducing them to chunking – when chunking you are saving memory space, so instead of memorizing 12 items you only may need to remember three chunks!

Packing your suitcase:

- Make a list of all the items you need to take with you – take your time with this and write them in any order.
- Now think of some main headings for these items, for example day clothes, house clothes, night clothes, washing items, brochures, travel information.
- Now select around four headings and put the items into those headings, for example:
  1. Clothes: day casual clothes, evening clothes, shoes.
  2. Toiletries and bed items.
  3. Correspondence items and entertainment: address book, pen for postcards, computer/tablet, books.
  4. Travel documents: passport, hotel information, flight and connections, tourist information.

Follow-up

You can get them to practise chunking with other items, for example for a school trip or school day.

Word toolbox

Note all the new words that are used. Depending on the age of the child, words like 'itinerary' or 'schedule' can be used.

Learning chart

Prompt your child to record their learning.

Today I learned _____

Additional resources

This website might be useful to begin with: www.verywellmind.com/chunking-how-can-this-technique-improve-your-memory-2794969

https://thepeakperformancecenter.com/educational-learning/thinking/chunking/chunking-as-a-learning-strategy

57. Fortunately and Unfortunately

Introduction

This activity can be useful for developing the executive functioning part of the brain, which involves a number of important aspects relating to thinking, evaluation, processing information and decision making. This activity requires consideration of options and predicting what might happen after an event. Practice at prediction can also help with reading comprehension.

Good for...

All ages but can be very useful for children in primary and secondary school.

Time frame

Allow at least one hour for this activity and do a follow-up at a future time.

Preparation/Materials

You might want to discuss with the child that there are two ways of looking at most things – good and bad! These are sometimes called pros and cons. So the child needs to be aware that when they make decisions there may be some disadvantages as well as advantages. This is also good practice for evaluation, which is seen as a higher-order skill. You may therefore want to start by giving some examples of your own that relate to family issues or the child's personal situation.

Teaching tip

It is a good idea to have lots of practice before your child does this activity. Try to relate the examples to everyday situations that they might experience.

Activity

Consider the statements below and complete them using both 'fortunately' and 'unfortunately'. An example is shown below:

1. The school bus was late this morning; *fortunately my friend's father passed in his car and gave me a lift to school.*
   The school bus was late this morning; *unfortunately I was very late for class and missed morning snack time.*
2. The large truck was loaded with frozen goods for the local supermarket; fortunately/ unfortunately _____

3. The football crowd shouted angrily; fortunately/unfortunately _____
_____

4. Mum asked me to put the bread into the brand-new toaster; fortunately/unfortunately
_____

5. The police officer yelled; fortunately/unfortunately _____

6. Our football game was stopped because the snow became very heavy; fortunately/
unfortunately _____

7. Without warning my bedroom light went out; fortunately/unfortunately _____
_____

8. My best friend is absent from school; fortunately unfortunately _____
_____

9. The new store had loads of computer games; fortunately/unfortunately _____
_____

10. My teacher gave the class extra maths homework; fortunately/unfortunately _____
_____

Follow-up

Try this with a group of friends – each person in the group has to say either 'fortunately' or 'unfortunately' to the statement.

Word toolbox

What words did your child learn today?

Learning chart

Prompt your child to record their learning.

Today I learned _____

Additional resources

There is a good explanation of executive functioning and dyslexia here: https://athome.readinghorizons.com/research/executive-functioning-and-dyslexia

58. Inferring Clues

Introduction

Children with dyslexia can often struggle with prediction and inferencing. Inferring clues or riddles can help these children develop their prediction skills and build their ability to practise interpreting figurative language, homophones and idioms. Not only does inferring clues and riddles help develop these skills, it provides a fun and challenging game for children and adults alike!

Good for...

Children of all ages.

Time frame

Anywhere from 10 minutes to 30 minutes.

Preparation/Materials

Printouts of the clues provided on heavy cardstock (see the Appendix).

Activity

Inferring Clues is an easy and fun activity to play anywhere. Take some time to print off the clues provided (see the Appendix) or research more from the links provided below. Cut out the cards and read the clues aloud to your child or your entire family. Read slowly and allow time for your child to think about the clues and make guesses.

Follow-up

For an added challenge, you can add a timing option and only allow a certain amount of time to answer the questions.

Additional resources/ideas

www.philtulga.com/Riddles.html
https://quizlet.com/76611235/inference-riddles-flash-cards
www.tinytap.it/activities/g29t/play/inferencing-with-riddles

CHAPTER 7

Learning Skills

We have mentioned quite a number of times in the introductions to the activities that we aim to help learners become aware of how they learn. Having this knowledge particularly as they advance further up the school can help children and young people take control of their own learning, their homework and the revision plans for exams. This chapter is about helping children identify their own learning preference and being able to use that to help them learn both effectively and efficiently.

We are not of the opinion that one particular style of learning is better for children with dyslexia but we appreciate that children will have a preference and it is important that they become aware of this. Knowing how they learn best – and this includes the learning environment – can help learners with dyslexia. They may not realize that having background music or using a small table lamp instead of a main ceiling light can help them learn more effectively. These things may not work for everyone but it is a good idea to try them out – experiment and take risks with learning.

Some of the activities in this chapter also look at exams and how to help your child use their abilities to the full. Self-knowledge provides a good avenue for this and indeed for lifelong learning.

ACTIVITIES

59. Draw Your Own Timeline

Introduction

Dates and facts are not everyone's strength. Often, we can remember dates but cease to remember why they are important or how they are interconnected. Anyone attending a history class can attest to this. Doodling or sketching facts and dates may be a way to visually cue our memories and help us study for tests or prepare for an exam or even help us write an essay. Young people with dyslexia often have superior visual skills and like and excel at drawing. Drawing a sequence is often more helpful than trying to orally recount events, as the act of sketching kinesthetically enables them to recall important information.

Good for...

A history class where a child has to remember a sequence or event that can be broken up into a chain of events that is a challenge to remember. Often, children and young people with dyslexia have trouble memorizing random dates and facts because many learners are visual learners. By drawing a timeline, they can create a visual cue for important facts and dates and use this picture to jog their memory and serve as a starting point for an essay question or a test.

Time frame

A timeline can be drawn in about 15–20 minutes and then used as an aid to study for a history test.

Preparation/Materials

Paper and a pencil. You may also want to include colourful markers or stickers to make the timeline more interesting. This will depend on the age/interest of your child.

Teaching tip

Timelines are wonderful study aids and really help students pare down larger pieces of information to the simple facts that summarize an event. Make sure when your child is creating their timeline that they use the who, what, when, where, why questions as a starting point to frame their symbols and dates as this will help them select only the relevant information to be learned.

It's important to revisit the timeline until your child can comfortably and easily recall events that make up a larger chunk of information.

Activity

Choose an event that has multiple steps or dates and facts to sequence. An example of a timeline might be the emergence of the Industrial Revolution. After reading about the event, have your child draw a line on a piece of paper. At either end of the line, they make a note of important dates to remember. In the space between these two dates, your child visually records important facts, dates, people or objects that will help them recreate the timeline of the Industrial Revolution. When they are choosing images and dates to include in the timeline, prompt them by asking questions such as who, what, when, where, why to frame what should and shouldn't be included. Once your child has captured all the images they would like, they can keep this picture and use it as a study aid for a test or exam. You can help your child by pointing to images and have them retell the scene to you.

Follow-up

This timeline can be used to study throughout the week before a test or as a prompt to frame a piece of writing.

Word toolbox

What words did your child learn today?

60. Snap It!

Introduction

Many children struggle with organizational skills and can often lose track of important dates. This can be the cause of much stress for both children and parents as they struggle at the last minute to get work done. This activity is a quick tool to help your child keep track of their assignments and prevent the homework slide! It also takes advantage of technology and can save a child the panic of having to copy notes from the board.

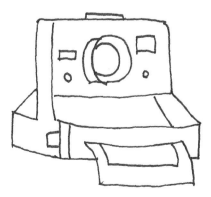

Good for...

Keeping track of assignment deadlines, doing homework assignments, developing organizational skills. This activity works best for secondary school students who have multiple classes and multiple deadlines.

Time frame

10 minutes a day; to be used at the end of each school day or in-between classes to keep track of assignments, test dates and project deadlines.

Preparation/Materials

- Smartphone
- Google Calendar

Teaching tip

Be sure to work with your child and teach them how to do this activity for themselves. The key to making this work is creating a routine that will allow them to organize themselves. Be consistent with time and place and help them for a set time period and then have them show you that they are able to keep track of this independently.

Activity

Have your child get in the habit of 'snapping' important information they may need for homework. In lieu of an organizer, teach your child how to record and take pictures at the end of the day so they can record assignments once they are home. Once your child is home from school, sit down with them and take all of the assignments and due dates and plug them into Google Calendar. This will help your child keep track of homework and ensure that it is complete. It is also good for organizing and chunking longer assignments into shorter, more manageable goals.

Follow-up

Once your child feels comfortable with using their phone to organize their schedule, challenge them to find five new ways to use other technology to help them with their organizational skills. For example, how can Siri help them?

Additional resources

www.ldonline.org/article/65104
www.youtube.com/watch?v=Zdw3tbeVy9M

61. Rebus Puzzles

Introduction

Children with dyslexia benefit greatly from engaging in activities that develop their reasoning skills and their vocabulary. Rebus Puzzles use strategically placed words and images that stand for a common phrase or saying or word. Trying their hand at these puzzles and even creating their own can be a fun activity but it can also help your child develop critical thinking and focus.

 ## Good for...
School-aged children.

Time frame

About five minutes to print out the provided Rebus Puzzles or 10–15 minutes to find additional Rebus Puzzles online. 20–30 minutes or more to solve the puzzles.

Preparation/Materials

- A printout of the Rebus Puzzles provided (see the Appendix)
- Scissors (if you wish to cut out the puzzles)
- Heavy cardstock

Activity

Print out the provided Rebus Puzzles and help your child solve them. The answer key is provided as well. There is a wealth of these puzzles available online for all levels. You can sit down with your child for a longer session of solving puzzles or you can have a daily Rebus for your family and post one puzzle up on your family bulletin board for family members to try to solve and think about throughout the day.

Follow-up

If the puzzle can't be solved, use that as an opportunity to learn about the common phrase or saying and its origins. Look it up online at one of the following sites:

www.boredpanda.com/origins-commonly-used-phrases-words-idioms/?utm_source=google&utm_medium=organic&utm_campaign=organic

www.history.com/news/10-common-sayings-with-historical-origins

http://www.bibliomania.com/2/3/255/frameset.html

Additional resources/ideas

For more Rebus Puzzle fun, check out these sites:

https://kids.niehs.nih.gov/games/brainteasers/rebus-puzzles/index.htm

www.rd.com/list/rebus-puzzles

www.fun-with-words.com/rebus_puzzles.html

62. Thinking Prompts

Introduction

It is important for reading comprehension and the overall development of learning skills to encourage children and young people to think deeply and broadly about what they are reading and learning about. Often children with dyslexia may skip this as they may want the task finished as quickly as possible or they may have difficulty in knowing where to start. This activity aims to encourage thinking skills by providing prompts to help learners make a start with this. It also encourages self-sufficiency and can lead to self-monitoring.

Good for...

Most learners, particularly those in the later stages of primary school and at secondary school.

Time frame

They can take as long as they wish for this – this type of activity should be practised periodically and is not a one-off task.

Preparation/Materials

Perhaps start with a discussion about the importance of thinking about and developing a task by looking at it from all angles. You can indicate that there may be more than one answer to any problem and that is why it is important to look at the question and consider different responses.

Teaching tip

Pre-task discussion is important for this so spend time discussing the different types of questions with the child.

Activity

For this activity, it is best that the child selects a piece of text or even a book that they have been working on. You then provide them with the different type of questions they can ask themselves. These include:

- **Literal questions –** for example, Can you tell me what happened? When/where/who? What are the main points in this text?
- **Inferential questions –** reading between the lines, drawing out conclusions which are based on, but go beyond, the information given in the text.
- **Deductive questions –** drawing conclusions from the information given throughout the text.
- **Justification –** finding evidence in the text to justify responses.

Follow-up

You can also give your child some points to help with the discussion and thinking, such as:

- What makes you think that?
- What do you think?
- What words give you that impression?
- How do you feel about…?
- Can you explain why…?
- Do you agree with …'s opinion?
- Do you like the bit where…?
- I wonder if…
- Is there anything that puzzles you?
- I'm not sure what I think about…
- I wonder what the writer intended…
- This bit reminds me of…
- I would hate to have that happen to me, wouldn't you?
- I like the way the writer has…
- Are there any patterns you notice (e.g. familiar story structure, images)?
- I wonder why the writer has decided to…

Word toolbox
What words did your child learn today?

Learning chart
Prompt your child to record their learning.

Today I learned _____

Additional resources

www.brighthorizons.com/family-resources/developing-critical-thinking-skills-in-children
www.parentingscience.com/teaching-critical-thinking.html

63. My Learning Preference

Introduction
It is important that learners with dyslexia are aware of their own learning preferences. The acquisition of a successful learning style can be an important determinant of successful learning – irrespective of the task, or the material to be learned. This includes all aspects of learning and particularly lesson planning, classroom design and the overall learning environment. This activity will help your child work out their own preferred learning style.

The points that need to be considered are:

- Cognition – how a child learns, memorizes information and attends.
- Social – whether they prefer working on their own or with others and their discussion preferences.
- Emotional – self-esteem, ability to persevere, level of frustration, level of enquiry skills and degree of control they have over their own learning.
- Physiological factors – time of day, food intake, water availability, sleep levels, need for movement when learning.

Good for...
All learners – some may need guidance to work out their style of learning.

Time frame

This can take around one hour.

Preparation/Materials

First, try to discuss what their own particular learning preference is, then do the activity.

 ## Teaching tip

It is important to note that there is no right or wrong answer and you need to reassure the child of this.

Activity

Using these questions, try to work out your child's learning preference.

Motivation

- What tasks and activities interest the learner?
- What kind of prompting and cueing is necessary to increase motivation?
- What kind of incentives motivate the learner – leadership opportunities, working with others, free time or physical activity?

Persistence

- Does the learner stick to a task until completion without breaks?
- Are frequent breaks necessary when working on difficult tasks?
- To what extent does the learner take responsibility for their own learning?
- Does the learner attribute success or failure to self or others?

Structure

- Are the learner's personal effects (desk, clothing, materials) well organized or cluttered?
- How does the learner respond to someone imposing organizational structure on them?

Social interaction

- When is the learner's best work accomplished – when working alone, with one other or in a small group?
- Does the learner ask for approval or need to have work checked frequently?

Modality preference

- What type of instructions does the learner most easily understand – written, oral or visual?
- Does the learner respond more quickly and easily to questions about stories heard or read?

Sequential or simultaneous learning

- Does the learner begin with one step and proceed in an orderly fashion or have difficulty following sequential information?
- Is there a logical sequence to the learner's explanations or do their thoughts bounce around from one idea to another?

Physical mobility

- Does the learner move around the room frequently or fidget when seated?
- Does the learner like to stand or walk while learning something new?

Time of day

- During which time of day is the learner most alert?
- Is there a noticeable difference between morning work completed and afternoon work?

Sound, light and temperature

- Does the learner seek out places that are particularly quiet?
- Does the learner like to work in dimly lit areas or say that the light is too bright?
- Does the learner leave their coat on when others seem warm?

Furniture design

- When given a choice, does the learner sit on the floor, lie down, or sit in a straight chair to read?

Follow-up

This activity is like an observation overview of the child's learning preference. You should note the responses to this and that will provide you with an idea of their learning preference.

Learning chart

Prompt your child to record their learning.

Today I learned _____

Additional resources

www.time4learning.com/learning-styles
www.parents.com/toddlers-preschoolers/development/intellectual/raising-kids-who-love-to-learn

64. Ready for Revision

Introduction

It is important to discuss revision and revision strategies with your child, regardless of age. The object of revision is similar to the object of learning – that is, *not* to memorize information, but rather to enhance understanding of the issues and to be able to develop important points in written work. The key to success for the person with dyslexia is organization. It is important that a study or revision plan is developed.

Good for...

Teens and those undertaking exams.

Time frame

No real time frame but it is worthwhile spending an hour on this.

Preparation/Materials

Your child can select a topic they are currently working on and this can be the focus of this activity. You will need:

- Pen or pencil
- Lined and blank paper
- Index cards
- (Optional) smartphone with a voice-activated app
- A blank mind map
- Time – do not rush this – it is very important

Teaching tip

It might be an idea to discuss this using different types of exam questions.

Activity

Help your child develop a programme of revision by identifying a number of steps. There is an example below and children should try this out first and perhaps make their own adjustments.

Step 1: Compile notes for the topic. That is, main facts and ideas.

Step 2: Write or dictate key points and issues using a voice-activated app. Try to reduce these to around five at most.

Step 3: Listen to information gathered on the recording without taking notes.

Step 4: Listen a second time but on this occasion, enter the information on a prepared mind map or any other form selected.

Step 5: Write linear notes from the mind map. Use the key points identified in Step 2 as headings and make your own notes under each.

Step 6: Put key words or phrases for each area on index cards. Try to keep this brief.

It must be remembered that revision is an active process, not a passive one, so it is important that your child does this themselves.

Follow-up

Get your child to make up their own steps and try this out with the same or a different topic.

Word toolbox

What words did your child learn today?

Learning chart

Prompt your child to record their learning.

Today I learned _____

Additional resources

www.readwritethink.org/parent-afterschool-resources/tips-howtos/help-child-edit-revise-30594.html
Good for young children: www.theconfidentteacher.com/2018/01/top-10-revision-strategies/good
strategies here for revision

65. Target: Reaching Your Goal

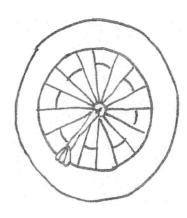

Introduction

At times, learning can seem to stretch out before a child with no clear goal of why they are learning what they do. Their learning should always contain an element of input or control. Goal or target setting is an excellent way to achieve this as well as adding an element of metacognition to a child's learning. By learning to set realistic targets and goals, children can become empowered by their learning and feel as though they have some control.

Good for...

Metacognition, self-esteem, resilience, engagement and motivation. This exercise is ideal for secondary school students. It can also be adapted for older primary school children.

Time frame

One month. Young people establish their goals at the beginning of the month and then at the end, reflect on their goals and targets to see how successful they were.

Preparation/Materials

- A printout of the Personal Goal Setting worksheet (see the Appendix)
- Pen, pencils, colouring pencils

Teaching tip

If you think that some external motivation could be helpful for your child, then go ahead and establish some criteria for this. Not all students are naturally internally motivated and they may require some incentives in order to achieve this. What is important about this exercise is that it is followed for a period of time in order for it to become a habit. If your child does not require any external motivation, then just work with them. Part of a child's learning process is to achieve a sense of mastery for the simple satisfaction of achievement. This is also a theme that requires work and steady input.

Activity

With your child, discuss the importance of targets and goal setting as a way of keeping us on track in all areas of our lives. When you set a target or goal, you are actively trying to achieve something and are more likely to be successful in achieving this goal if you are conscientiously participating in it. On the sheet supplied, ask your child to fill out goals they have for a one-month time period. The goals should be related to something they would like to achieve in their learning or in their daily habits. Some examples might be: doing my homework every night independently, packing my own lunch, reading for 20 minutes every night before going to bed, being a neater printer, not talking so much in class, having a tidier desk at home and at school. This list is not exhaustive but gives you an idea of some of the elements that can be included in the goals.

After your child establishes some goals, it's important to fill in the section on how they will achieve these goals. They must think of real-life steps they can take in order to achieve their goals. Without these steps, goal setting becomes too abstract and difficult to achieve.

Finally, at the end of the month, ask your child to look back at their goals and record if they were successful or not. They need to be detailed as to why or why not they achieved a goal and recognize what they did in order to achieve it. Once they have reflected on their goals, they then colour in the target according to how successful they were. This cycle can then be repeated and a new series of goals established to help them in their learning.

Follow-up

Once you have successfully reached your individual targets, try a family target challenge or perhaps propose a class target challenge to your teacher. Also, if you feel comfortable, you can try a daily challenge and keep a diary of how successful you were. Through practice, setting targets and goals will become second nature and part of your daily life.

Additional resources

www.parents.com/parenting/better-parenting/style/how-to-teach-kids-perseverance-goal-setting

66. The Learning Gym: Develop Your Strengths

Introduction

It is a good idea to try to relate learning to a gym for PE. You go to the gym to keep your body in shape so a learning gym keeps your brain in shape. You therefore need to exercise your brain just as you exercise your body. You might want to start by giving your child some key points about learning; for example:

1. Spend time making sure you understand the topic.
2. Make a learning plan – what resources do you need?
3. Give yourself targets and a time frame.
4. Think of what you have covered previously in this topic.
5. Monitor your progress – keep a note of what you have done and what you still want to do.
6. Think how you can reinforce the ideas and the materials you are learning – this is called overlearning and is important for learners with dyslexia.
7. Think of some recap activities – revision.
8. Try to use the new materials in discussion or in written work – use it to make sure you don't lose it!
9. Remember to use all your skills, particularly visual skills. Active learning – that is, doing something or experiencing it as well as discussing it – works best for learners with dyslexia.
10. Try out some memory strategies to find out what works best for you.

Good for...

All learners in the upper stages of primary school and all secondary school students.

Time frame

Do not rush this as this is a blueprint that they can refer to with different types of learning.

Preparation/Materials

Pre-discussion is important – it is a good idea to start by asking your child how they learn and take it from there.

Teaching tip

Discussion is important for this and also to look at some examples of how the learner has used and adapted this.

Activity

Discuss the key points given above with the child and then get them to practise these with some topics they are learning. They can copy the key points into their notebook and use them as a checklist.

Follow-up

It is important to practise these so the follow-up should be for the child to use this formula with new topics and review how successful they have been. At this stage, they can make changes but the important point is that they have taken some ownership of their own learning.

Word toolbox

What words did your child learn today?

Learning chart

Prompt your child to record their learning.

Today I learned _____

Additional resources

Good for motivation for learning: www.educationcorner.com/motivating-your-child-to-learn.html

Key phrases here – value the process over the product: www.nytimes.com/guides/smarterliving/
help-your-child-succeed-at-school67

67. Step Up! Planning for Events and Goal Setting

Introduction

Building on the idea of goal setting, helping learners plan for important events or goals and setting targets for these specific events helps them to develop their reasoning and planning skills and will enable them to research and learn the steps they need to take to complete a larger-scale task. These are invaluable skills for learners throughout their lives.

Good for...

Children at secondary school. It will help in metacognition, intrinsic and extrinsic motivation, resilience and self-esteem.

Time frame

This can vary from one week to months based on what the goal or event is and the steps required to complete the task.

Preparation/Materials

- Pens or pencils
- A printout of the My Goal Planner worksheet (see the Appendix)
- Computer or access to a computer for research
- Notepad for brainstorming

Teaching tip

It's a good idea to be somewhat of a coach for your child for this activity. If you find that your child is very motivated, you may be the one to work with them to set up the goal success planning and then once they have the steps, they will be on their way. If they are not as motivated, you may play a bigger role and need to provide incentives to help them achieve success. It's a good idea to gauge where your child is on the motivation spectrum and make a note of this.

Activity

As children get older, they start to develop their own ideas and their own wants and desires for their lives. Things such as getting a driver's licence or learning to play a musical instrument are bigger goals that require preparation and planning. Learners who struggle with executive functioning can often feel lost and overwhelmed when looking at these goals. Helping them plan for these things by breaking the process down into small and manageable tasks will help them feel more successful and will ultimately help them achieve their goal.

If your child has a specific event or goal they are wanting to reach, you're ready to use the provided My Goal Planner. If they aren't sure about what goals they might want to reach for, have them brainstorm their ideas on a blank notepad. Once your child has targeted a specific goal (e.g. getting their driver's licence), have them write their goal at the top of the page. It's a good idea think about what you want the outcome to be and then work backwards to see how you will get there by considering your strategy, the things you will need (both physical and mental) and the steps you will need to take. This might require researching the task to see how others have done it in the past or what is required. Using 'getting a driver's licence' as an example, let's break the process down into steps for the young person:

Step 1: State your goal (I want to get my driver's licence).

Step 2: State the strategy (I will study for my learner's licence and will practise driving every day).

Step 3: State the things you will need to reach your goal (what is required to get a driver's licence, driver's licence study book, my computer to take quizzes on driving, access to a car, help from parents or guardians to drive with me when I practise, time to set aside for practising).

Step 4: Break down the process into manageable steps from start to finish (get driver's licence study book, study one chapter per day, take online quizzes if applicable, make appointment for learner's licence application, etc.).

Step 5: Check off tasks as they are completed.

Step 6: Reflect on your progress. How did you do? Did you meet your goal? What worked? What didn't work? Use these learning points as helpful tips for your next goal or event.

Follow-up

If you find that your child is not intrinsically motivated (doesn't tend to have the internal motivation to achieve goals), you might want to incorporate some external motivations to help them develop their own motivation. These could include providing incentives for them such as access to the car on a regular basis should they get their driver's licence. Not all children have intrinsic motivation so we can help them by providing some external tools to help them develop the motivation.

68. Create and Set Up Routines

Introduction

It is widely known that children who have learning difficulties or who have been diagnosed with attention deficit hyperactivity disorder (ADHD) can struggle with managing daily tasks and recognizing time limits. Even getting out of the house each morning can be a difficult task. Providing a framework for your child like a detailed and regular routine can help them to stay on task and be mindful of what they need to get done throughout the day.

Good for...

Setting up routines for children of all ages. Using pictures as well as words can be effective for younger children and using a more detailed chart can be effective for older children. This can be good for children of all abilities as routine setting can give them some control over their own schedules and help them achieve a sense of accomplishment as they complete their tasks.

Time frame

This should be a five-day routine, Monday to Friday, and you can allocate around 30 minutes to an hour to discuss and set up the different routines.

Preparation/Materials

- A printout of the worksheets about routines (see the Appendix)
- Markers or pencil crayons
- Laminator or access to a laminator (optional)
- Poster paper or cardstock
- Computer or access to a computer for research

Teaching tip

This is another activity where you can take on the role of coach with your child. Allow this activity to be an opportunity for you and your child to work as a team to develop routines that you both can agree on. This will help your child buy into the process and will set them up for success.

Activity

The most important thing about this activity is to think about and brainstorm the routines for your family and your children. Every family is structured differently and they have different routines that work for them. Take some time to think about what routines work for your family and jot them down. Think about the approximate times that they will complete these tasks and make a note of them. Also take into consideration, the age of your children and what types of routines they will need. We have included some sample routines for younger and older children. Feel free to use these if they fit with your family. If not, feel free to create your own! To make your routine chart more durable and long-lasting, laminate it using your laminator or have it laminated at your local printing store.

Once you have decided on the routine for your child, print out the provided routines or create your own just by writing them down on poster paper or cardstock and posting them on your family bulletin board or on some wall space in a common area of your home.

Putting the routines up is only one step to this process, however. Take some time to go over the routine with your child and discuss the steps for them. Instruct them to check their schedule daily and throughout the day to ensure they are keeping on task. Have them check off tasks as they complete them. This will help them feel a sense of accomplishment throughout the day.

Follow-up

You can extend this activity for your older children by creating a similar but more detailed routine that they can keep with them. Planners are a great way to encourage your children to set up and maintain a personal schedule for themselves.

69. A Musical Finale

Introduction

Some children with dyslexia can be very musical and they may have a good ear for music, but quite often they have difficulty in reading music. This can be quite frustrating and they usually compensate by being excellent at playing using their musical intuition and by ear.

This activity provides some tips on reading music that you can try at home with your child.

Good for...

Children of all ages.

Preparation

Try to locate a musical score that your child is currently working on – or a popular everyday type of song.

Teaching tip

It is important that this does not de-skill your child as many successful musicians play by ear, but it is a good idea to get into the habit of reading the music score. Try a small piece at a time and try to ensure it is a tune your child is familiar with.

Activity

Reading music involves sequencing and tracking skills, so the key aspects of the music need to be highlighted. You can try this approach using colour combinations for all scales and different notes. It is a good idea to print out the type of notes in the colour you have selected for that note. You can also make the stave music sheet bigger by photocopying it in a larger size.

For sequencing and tracking, use larger scores so it is easier for the child to track. You can also try a coloured overhead transparency as this might reduce the glare and help with sequencing.

Break the music sheet into sections and do not provide the full page at the same time.

When you decide on colours for different notes, do this in discussion with your child – allow them to choose the colours.

Follow-up

Have a look at this website to reinforce this strategy: www.smartiesforbrass.com

Word toolbox

What words did your child learn today?

Additional resources

The British Dyslexia Association has an excellent music committee: www.bdadyslexia.org.uk

70. Know Your Word Toolbox

Introduction

Your child will have collected lots of words throughout this book. This is now the opportunity to arrange them and try to consolidate the meaning of these words. It was anticipated that all or most of the words are new to them. So the idea of this final activity is to consolidate these words and ensure that they know their meanings. Overlearning is important for all children with dyslexia. They will have used these words in the activities so now they have to put them into a chart with the meanings.

Activity: my toolbox words

Your child needs to make a chart like the one below using the words they have put into their word toolbox in each activity. They need to write the meaning and a sentence using the word. Two examples are shown below – a word for younger children and one for more advanced learners.

Word	Meaning	Sentence
Explain	To give a reason for something	The teacher had to explain the maths problem very clearly to the class.
Paraphrase	To rewrite a piece of text using different words	The sentence was too difficult for the student so I had to paraphrase it.

Well done!

Concluding Comments

We hope you have found this book a useful resource and that the activities fit in with your child's needs. We appreciate that parenting children with dyslexia is not easy as they can be quite resistant at times to new learning and may be reluctant to work on those areas they find challenging. As we indicated in the 'How to Use this Book' it is a good idea to use this book to 'dip into' and the activities can be accessed in any order.

The golden rule for helping children and young people with dyslexia is to make the activities as multisensory as possible – that is, visual, auditory, kinesthetic and tactile. We have tried to incorporate this methodology into all our activities in some way.

Another tip we can give you at this stage is to listen to your child. We are sure you do that, but it is not uncommon for children with dyslexia to try to cover up and pretend they are understanding the task, when in fact they are not.

There is also a great deal of research on the emotional side of dyslexia – see the chapter by Penny Ashton (2021) in Gillian Ashley's book, *Parenting a Dyslexic Child*. Penny highlights the importance of self-esteem for children with dyslexia and indicates that a healthy self-esteem can aid the child a great deal in reaching their full potential. It is important to discuss this with the school, but parents can also help their children believe in themselves. This can be achieved through success; it does not have to be major successes but small positive 'points' – a 'good work' comment as they work on their homework can do the trick. Self-esteem is something children feel – you can't buy it, you can't give it to them, they have to feel it! That is why it is a good idea to work in harmony with the school since your child will spend a great deal of their day at school.

We are, of course, hoping that teachers will also use this book and together the activities can be shared between home and school.

It is also worth mentioning that although the challenges associated with dyslexia can be a major obstacle for the child at school, there will be positive aspects to your child's profile. While accessing print may be challenging, other areas, perhaps investigation skills or creative tasks, may be a significant strength. There are many accounts of famous people who are dyslexic and have been able to overcome their challenges by using their strengths. Indeed, in most professions, including university professors, medical doctors, vets, lawyers, architects and engineers and many more, you will find people with dyslexia. Some famous authors, TV personalities and well-known film producers are dyslexic (see the website of the Helen Arkell Dyslexia Charity[1]).

The message is simple: never give up! We, as authors of this activity book and practising professionals with years of experience in this area, know first-hand that success is achievable and that it may take longer – or it may not – but it will come in some form. We are also conscious of the fact that we are working with individual children, and their needs are therefore very individual. The common element may well be their dyslexia but the exceptional element is that they are unique. That is something to nurture and treasure. We hope this book has helped you achieve this and has helped your child to realize their potential and, most of all, enjoy learning!

1   www.helenarkell.org.uk/about-dyslexia/famous-dyslexics.php

Appendix

Chapter 2

1. Popcorn Reading

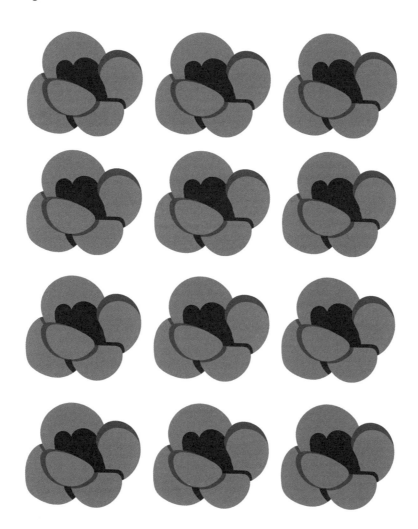

2. Mouse and Cheese Reading

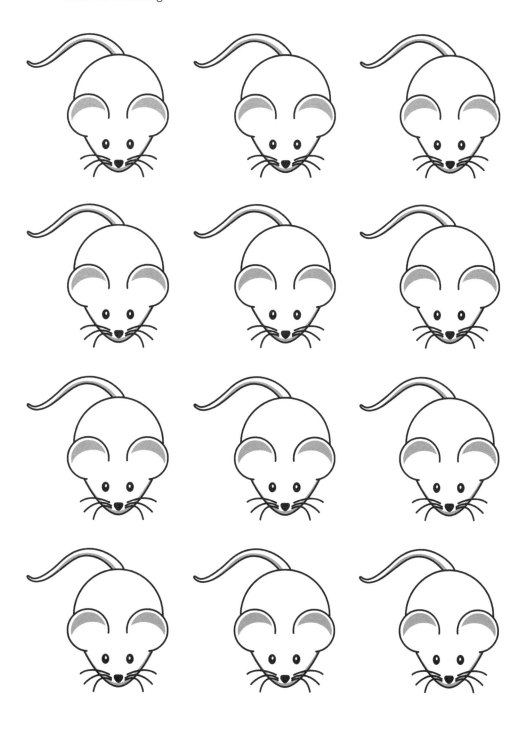

8. Story Sticks

9. Fortune Tellers

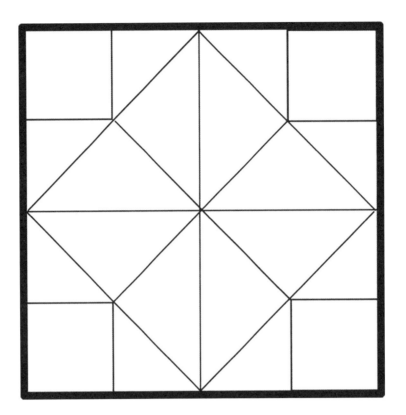

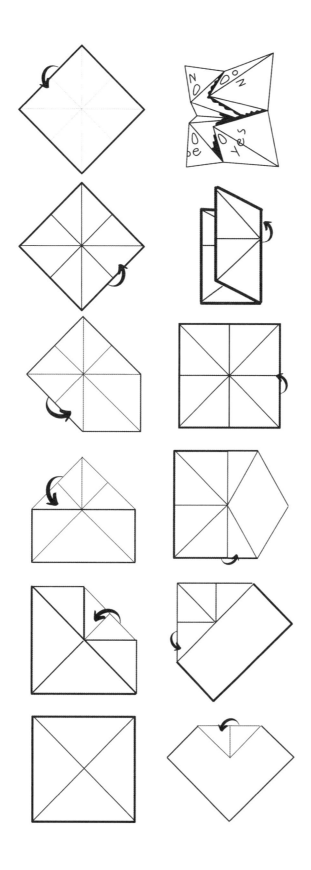

Chapter 3

13. Sentence Roll

NOUNS		VERBS		ADJECTIVE		WHERE?	
2	alien	2	crawl	2	stinky	2	bath
3	sloth	3	swim	3	yucky	3	attic
4	clown	4	jump	4	mushy	4	moon
5	zombie	5	flip	5	purple	5	circus
6	squid	6	squish	6	sleepy	6	treehouse
7	monster	7	yank	7	saggy	7	store
8	spider	8	yell	8	muddy	8	river
9	robot	9	wiggle	9	dirty	9	mudbog
10	alligator	10	squirm	10	chubby	10	cave
11	shark	11	waddle	11	squishy	11	bathroom
12	monkey	12	skate	12	chewy	12	garden

Nouns (person/thing)	Verb (action)	Adjective (describe the noun)	Where?

Write your sentence below:

_____

....

_____

_____

....

_____

_____

....

_____

Draw your sentence below:

14. List It!

List It!

4 things you find on a sports field	9 items you would find in a supermarket	8 body parts
10 things you would find in a classroom		Miss a Turn
5 parts on a bicycle		any 4 vowels
Miss a Turn		10 colours
8 animals you would find in a zoo	any 4 capital cities in the world	7 letters of the alphabet
7 toppings you would put on a pizza	Trade places with opponent	5 ways to use water
5 things you would put in a fish tank		Miss a Turn

4 types of prehistoric animals · 6 types of fruit · 5 things with a frame

5 things that whistle · 7 letters of the alphabet · 5 ways to use water

6 things you can make with wood

FINISH!

START

16. Noun and Verb Charades

Noun and Verb Charades

book	dog	hat	monster	phone	ball
pen	cat	elephant	hamburger	bicycle	guitar
computer	car	lion	photograph	helmet	drums
eyeball	mouth	floor	window	idea	watch
shirt	shovel	heart	shoes	flower	skates
baking	running	jumping	sleeping	typing	lifting
biking	writing	driving	skating	skiing	gardening
swimming	drumming	whistling	climbing	dancing	cooking
singing	hugging	reading	boxing	eating	hiding
drinking	skipping	laughing	yelling	knitting	flying

20. Character on Social Media

FakeBook   Friends   Applications   Inbox (1)   Home

Profile Picture

Information

Relationship Status:

Current City:

Birthday:

Place of Work:

Friends

Likes

Posts

Update Status

_____
_____
_____
_____
_____
_____

Life Events

_____
_____
_____
_____
_____
_____
_____
_____
_____
_____
_____
_____

Chapter 4

31. Spin It and Write It!

8
2
1
3
5
7
4
6

_____

_____

_____

_____

_____

_____

_____

_____

_____

_____

_____

_____

_____

_____

32. Rainbow Word Spelling

33. Spelling Sleuths

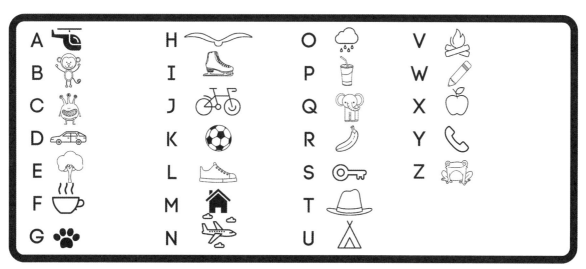

Become a spelling sleuth and create a secret code for your spelling words.

Example: you = 📞☁🏕

_____ _____ _____ _____

_____ _____ _____ _____

_____ _____ _____ _____

_____ _____ _____ _____

_____ _____ _____ _____

_____ _____ _____ _____

_____ _____ _____ _____

_____ _____ _____ _____

Chapter 5

37. Self-Care Checklist

MY SELF-CARE
Checklist
THINGS I CAN DO FOR MYSELF

☐ _____

☐ _____

☐ _____

☐ _____

☐ _____

☐ _____

☐ _____

41. Wall of Worries and Wall of Wisdom

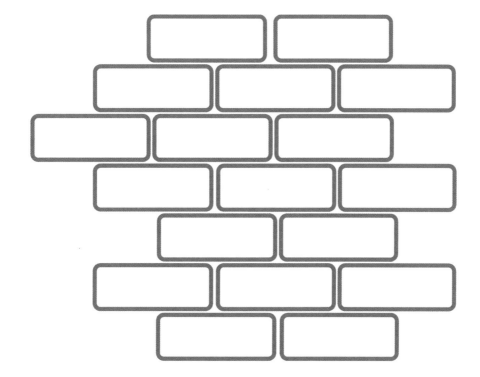

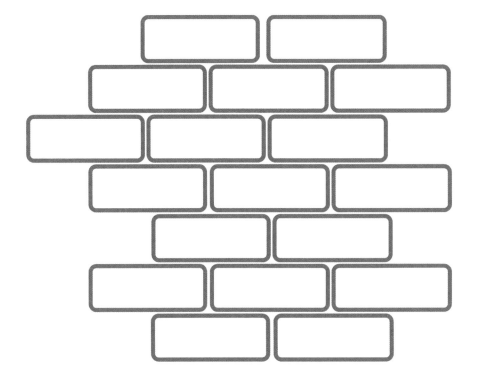

43. Pump, Pedal, Glide

Pump, Pedal, Glide

 Tasks that take effort – Strategies I can use to make the task easier	 Tasks that are easier for me – Strategies I can use to keep me engaged	Tasks that are easy for me – Strategies I can use to enjoy them

45. Family Values Board

OUR FAMILY VALUES

tell the truth ★ Challenge yourself

Learn something new

HONOUR YOUR FEELINGS

HELP EACH OTHER ♡ be kind

Make lots of mistakes

HAVE FUN! Play with LEGO®

ASK FOR HELP

Listen to Music ♪

live and love with your whole heart

Chapter 6

46. Organizing Passport

My Morning Passport

	MON	TUES	WED	THUR	FRI	SAT	SUN
BRUSH MY HAIR	○	○	○	○	○	○	○
BRUSH MY TEETH	○	○	○	○	○	○	○
WASH MY FACE	○	○	○	○	○	○	○
GET DRESSED	○	○	○	○	○	○	○
MAKE MY BED	○	○	○	○	○	○	○
PACK MY BAG (CHECK HOMEWORK AND SUPPLIES)	○	○	○	○	○	○	○
EAT BREAKFAST	○	○	○	○	○	○	○

My Evening Passport

	MON	TUES	WED	THUR	FRI	SAT	SUN
HAVE AN AFTERSCHOOL SNACK	◯	◯	◯	◯	◯	◯	◯
RELAX FOR 15 MINUTES	◯	◯	◯	◯	◯	◯	◯
DO MY HOMEWORK	◯	◯	◯	◯	◯	◯	◯
DO MY CHORES	◯	◯	◯	◯	◯	◯	◯
EAT DINNER	◯	◯	◯	◯	◯	◯	◯
BRUSH MY TEETH	◯	◯	◯	◯	◯	◯	◯

50. Frame It!

Frame It!

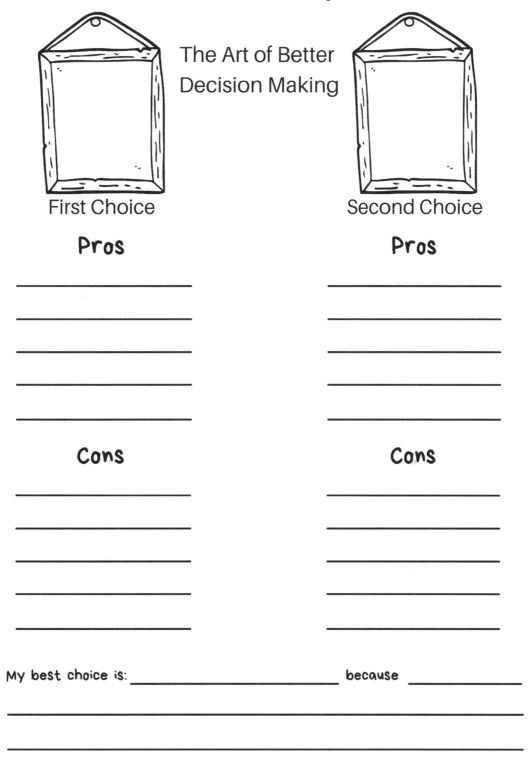

The Art of Better Decision Making

First Choice

Second Choice

Pros

Pros

_____

_____

_____

_____

_____

_____

_____

_____

_____

_____

Cons

Cons

_____

_____

_____

_____

_____

_____

_____

_____

My best choice is: _____ because _____

_____

_____

51. Tag It! Backpack Tags

My BagTag Checklist

- Check for homework
- Books and/or binders for homework
- Lunch bag
- Gym clothes
- _____
- _____

My BagTag Checklist

- _____
- _____
- _____
- _____
- _____
- _____
- _____

58. Inferring Clues

Birds fly south for me.

I am a season after autumn

Snow is common when I'm around.

WHAT AM I?

You can plant me.

You can pop me.

You can eat me on the cob.

WHAT AM I?

I can be peeled.

I am yellow.

You can make bread with me.

WHAT AM I?

I have a face.

I have hands.

I tell time.

WHAT AM I?

You can knock on me.

You can open me.

I can be slammed shut.

WHAT AM I?

I lie around all day.

You can walk all over me.

I can keep your feet warm.

WHAT AM I?

I have big ears.

I have an excellent memory.

My nose is long.

WHAT AM I?

I have an office.

I don't sit at a desk.

You can come to me when you're sick.

WHO AM I?

I AM WINTER

I AM CORN

I AM A BANANA

I AM A CLOCK

I AM A DOOR

I AM A RUG

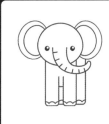

I AM AN ELEPHANT

I AM A DOCTOR

I have big ears.

I have a pouch.

I live Down Under.

WHAT AM I?

I transport people.

I can have one or two wheels.

I do not have an engine.

WHAT AM I?

I am slippery.

I can be fast.

You can slide down me.

WHAT AM I?

I can be turned on and off.

I help you see.

I make things brighter.

WHAT AM I?

I tell you when a guest arrives.

I am loud.

I can be rung.

WHAT AM I?

You can see through me.

You put me on your face.

I help you see better.

WHAT AM I?

You can open me.

I provide hours of entertainment.

I am full of words.

WHAT AM I?

I live in space.

I shine at night.

I have different phases.

WHAT AM I?

I AM A KANGAROO

I AM A BICYCLE OR UNICYCLE

I AM A SLIDE

I AM A LIGHT

I AM A DOORBELL

I AM EYEGLASSES

I AM A BOOK

I AM THE MOON

Chapter 7

61. Rebus Puzzles

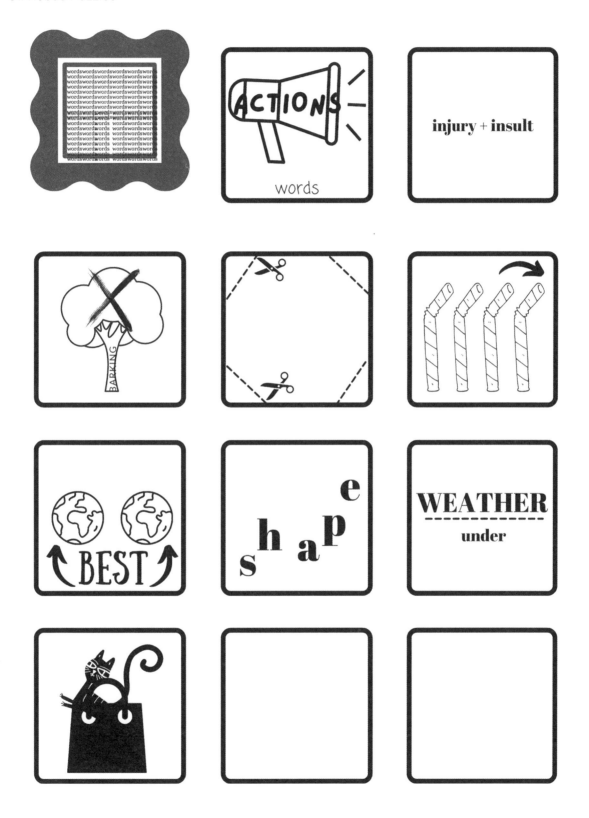

Answer: A picture is worth a thousand words

Answer: Actions speak louder than words

Answer: Add insult to injury

Answer: Barking up the wrong tree

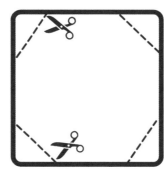

Answer: Cutting corners

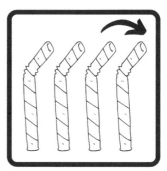

Answer: That's the last straw

Answer: The best of both worlds

Answer: Bent out of shape

Answer: Under the weather

Answer: Let the cat out of the bag

65. Target: Reaching Your Goal

Target!
Personal Goal Setting

Three goals I would like to work on this month:

1 ....

2 ....

3 ....

Three steps I need to take to achieve my goals:

1 ....

2 ....

3 ....

How did I do?

....

....

....

67. Step Up! Planning for Events and Goal Setting

My Goal Planner

The Goal:

The Strategy:

Steps to Take:

- ▪ _____
- ▪ _____
- ▪ _____
- ▪ _____
- ▪ _____
- ▪ _____
- ▪ _____
- ▪ _____
- ▪ _____

What do I need to reach my goal?

Reflect – How did I do?

68. Create and Set Up Routines

My Morning Routine

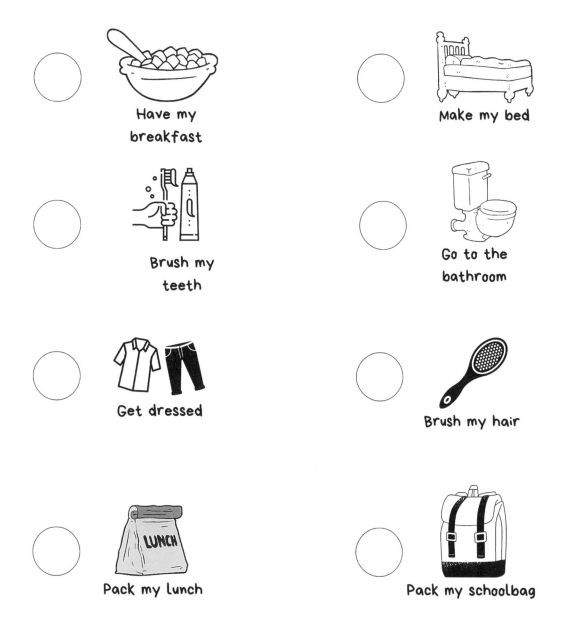

Have my breakfast

Make my bed

Brush my teeth

Go to the bathroom

Get dressed

Brush my hair

Pack my lunch

Pack my schoolbag

My Daily Routine

7:00 am	Morning Routine	Make bed, brush teeth, have breakfast
8:00 am	Prepare for School	Pack lunch, pack schoolbag
9:00 am to 3:00pm	School Time	
3:30 pm	Have Snack	
4:00 pm	Do Homework	
7:00 pm	Reading	
8:30 pm	Bedtime Routine	Brush teeth, put on pajamas

My Evening Routine

Do my homework

Have my snack

Have my dinner

Read a book

Clean up my dishes

Brush my teeth

Put my pajamas on

Further Information

Contacts

British Dyslexia Association: www.bdadyslexia.org.uk
Dyslexia Scotland: www.dyslexiascotland.org.uk
Northern Ireland Dyslexia Association: www.nidyslexiacentre.co.uk
Dyslexia Association of Ireland: www.dyslexia.ie
Dyslexia Scotland: www.dyslexiascotland.org.uk
Dyslexia Action: www.dyslexiaaction.org.uk
Helen Arkell Dyslexia Charity: www.arkellcentre.org.uk
Lighthouse Learning Centre Cairo: www.llcegypt.com
International Dyslexia Association: www.interdys.org

Professional Association of Teachers of Students with SpLDs: www.patoss-dyslexia.org
Real Training – distance learning, face-to-face training and consultancy to education professionals: https://realtraining.co.uk
Council for the Registration of Schools Teaching Dyslexic Pupils: https://crested.org.uk
Dyslexia Canada: www.dyslexiacanada.org
The Literacy Intervention and Training (LIT) Group: www.thelitgroup.ca
REACH Learning Centre: www.reachlearningcentre.com
Canadian Academy of Therapeutic Tutors: www.ogtutors.com

Online resources

www.dysguise.com/free-resources – superb free resources from this website on reading, spelling, writing, maths and memory. There is also a section on classroom support strategies.

www.drgavinreid.com/free-downloads – free downloads on overview of research, signposts for inclusion, effective learning, teaching strategies and ideas for parents.

www.bdadyslexia.org.uk/educator – this British Dyslexia Association site has resources and information for parents, employers, educators and dyslexic people themselves. There is a comprehensive list of frequently asked questions about dyslexia. For example, the hints and tips section for the primary school contains information on written work, reading, numeracy, time, skills, behaviour and practical aids. It also looks at speed of processing, poor concentration, difficulty following instructions, forgetful of words.

www.readingrockets.org/article/top-10-resources-dyslexia – lots of information on dyslexia.

www.helpingchildrenwithdyslexia.com – *Helping Children with Dyslexia: 21 Super Strategies to Ensure Your Child's Success at School* by Liz Dunoon.

www.stevechinn.co.uk/publications.html – *The Trouble with*

Maths: A Practical Guide to Helping Learners with Numeracy Difficulties by Steve Chinn.

www.crossboweducation.com – Crossbow Educational.

www.senbooks.co.uk – SEN books.

www.thedyslexiashop.co.uk – The Dyslexia Shop.

www.scoilnet.ie – Irish site with content for primary and secondary level, worksheets and revision activities for many subjects.

www.skoool.ie – Irish interactive learning website, with lots of secondary-level subject-specific content.

www.bbc.co.uk/learning – comprehensive online learning resources for all ages, including the Bitesize series of revision activities.

www.bbc.co.uk/skillswise – factsheets, worksheets, quizzes and games to help improve English and maths skills.

www.crayola.com – lesson plans, arts and crafts ideas and colouring pages.

www.teach-nology.com/worksheets/math – lots of free maths worksheets and more.

www.enchantedlearning.com – some free learning resources, lesson plans and worksheets. More available if you subscribe.

www.superkids.com – worksheets on maths, telling the time,

building vocabulary, logic and reasoning, and hangman games.

www.firstschoolyears.co.uk – free worksheets, flashcards and resources for primary literacy, maths and other subjects.

www.skillsworkshop.org – literacy and numeracy resources and worksheets for adults.

www.free-phonics-worksheets.com – free phonics worksheets.

www.dyslexiacentre.co.uk and www.nessy.co.uk – free learning worksheets, and free demo version of Nessy learning programme.

www.teflgames.com/games.html – games and quizzes to build vocabulary and word knowledge.

www.janbrett.com – free activities, worksheets, colouring pages and projects to download.

www.primaryresources.co.uk/index.htm – free lesson plans, activities and worksheets on many subjects.

www.senteacher.org/Files – printable worksheets and free software downloads (basic and special education).

www.rhlschool.com – English and maths worksheets to download.

www.discovery.com – Discovery Channel website, useful for science, history, geography, with lots of interactive games, puzzles and quizzes.

www.gutenberg.org – over 25,000 free ebooks available to download.

Free typing tutors

www.powertyping.com
www.learn2type.com

www.sense-lang.org/typing

More information

www.understood.org/en/learning-attention-issues/child-learning-disabilities/dyslexia/understanding-dyslexia – lots of information on the background to dyslexia.

www.callscotland.org.uk/information/dyslexia – excellent information on dyslexia.

www.callscotland.org.uk/information/dyslexia/hamish-story– Hamish's Story – Using iPads in School.

References that you may find useful

Aston, P. (2021) 'Supporting your Child's Emotional Development.' In G. Ashley (ed.) *Parenting A Dyslexic Child* (pp.161–188). London: Jessica Kingsley Publishers.

Cochrane, K. (2021) 'How Dyslexia is Diagnosed and Why it is Important.' In G. Ashley (ed.) *Parenting a Dyslexic Child* (pp.59–74). London: Jessica Kingsley Publishers.

Gordon, A. (2021) 'Top Tips from the Perspective of Someone with Dyslexia.' In G. Ashley (ed.) *Parenting A Dyslexic Child* (pp.37–46). London: Jessica Kingsley Publishers.

Henry, M.K. (2010) *Unlocking Literacy: Effective Decoding and Spelling Instruction* (second edition). Baltimore, MD: Brookes Publishing Co.

Kilpatrick, D.A. (2015) *Essentials of Assessing, Preventing and Overcoming Reading Difficulties*. New York, NY: Wiley.

Moats, L.C. (2020) *Speech to Print: Language Essentials for Teachers* (third edition). Baltimore, MD: Brookes Publishing Co.

National Institute of Child Health and Human Development (2000) *Report of the National Reading Panel. Teaching children to read: An evidence-based assessment of the scientific research literature on reading and its implications for instruction*. Reports of the subgroup. Washington, DC: U.S. Government Printing Office.

Reid, G. (2016) *Dyslexia: A Practitioner's Handbook* (fifth edition). New York, NY: Wiley.

Reid, G. and Guise, J. (2019) *Assessment for Dyslexia and Learning Differences: A Concise Guide for Teachers and Parents*. London: Jessica Kingsley Publishers.

Rose, J. (2006) Independent *Review into the Teaching of Early Reading*. London: Department for Education and Skills. https://dera.ioe.ac.uk/5551/2/report.pdf

Rose, J. (2009) *Identifying and Teaching Children and Young People with Dyslexia and Literacy Difficulties*. London: Department for Children, Schools and Families.

Shaywitz, S. (2009) *Overcoming Dyslexia: A New and Complete Science-Based Program for Reading Problems at Any Level* (revised edition). New York, NY: Alfred Knopf.

Velluntino, F., Fletcher, J., Snowling, M. and Scanlon, D. (2004) 'Specific reading disability (dyslexia): what have we learned in the past four decades?' *Journal of Child Psychology and Psychiatry*, 45(1), 2–40.

About the Authors

Gavin Reid

Gavin is an international psychologist and author. He was formerly a classroom teacher (10 years) and university lecturer (16 years). He was a senior lecturer at Moray House School of Education, University of Edinburgh from 1991 to 2007, where he wrote the first master's course in dyslexia in the UK in 1993. He has written over 35 books in the field of dyslexia, learning skills and motivation. His books have been translated into seven languages and some are in third, fourth and fifth editions.

Gavin, as a parent of a young man with significant learning issues, is committed to supporting parents in every way and has given lectures and seminars to parent groups throughout the UK and in many other countries.

He feels that one of the keys to success for children with dyslexia is effective communication between home and school and at the same time equipping parents with the knowledge and the confidence to advocate for their child in every way.

He has also spent a great deal of his working life developing and implementing teacher education programmes in dyslexia at all levels as well as running courses for parents.

Gavin is passionate about helping to achieve equal opportunities for those with dyslexia and other learning differences and is a strong advocate of the strengths and positive aspects of dyslexia. His website is www.drgavinreid.com

Michelle McIntosh

Michelle is a certified structured literacy supervisor and practitioner, Multisensory Structured Language Education (MSLE) instructor and supervising mentor for other structured literacy practitioners. Michelle sits on the Canadian Academy of Therapeutic Tutors as the Communications Director and Evaluations Supervisor. She has co-authored an educators' book series in the areas of structured literacy, reading fluency and written expression.

Michelle has over 10 years of experience helping students with varying learning difficulties, including dyslexia, dysgraphia and more. While helping those with these challenges, Michelle has become particularly interested in the social and emotional development of these students. As a parent of two boys, Michelle has a keen interest in learning and the social emotional impact having learning challenges can have. As such, Michelle has studied mindfulness, co-active coaching and trauma-sensitive education. Michelle holds a Co-Active Life Coaching certificate and has completed the Mindfulness for Educators course through Mindful Schools.

Michelle is passionate about helping students with learning difficulties to achieve success in literacy while also providing a safe and nurturing learning space where they can maintain their self-esteem, confidence and the knowledge that they can achieve anything.

Jenn Clark

Jenn is a certified structured literacy practitioner with a private practice in Vancouver, Canada. A certified primary school teacher, English as an Additional Language (EAL) instructor and Multisensory Structured Language Education (MSLE) instructor, she holds a certificate in competence in educational testing (CCET) and has spent the past 10 years teaching students with learning differences. She is co-creator of Aduri – a mindfulness programme for young children – and has co-authored several books on reading fluency, spelling and writing. She enjoys supporting children with dyslexia as well as assisting families, parents and schools with advocating for the rights of those with dyslexia.

Index